Amy Thomson.

BUSINESS SYSTEMS
for leisure and tourism

BUSINESS SYSTEMS
for leisure and tourism

SUE CUNDELL

PROJECT MANAGER: JOHN EDMONDS
PROJECT CONSULTANT: DEBBIE BETTERIDGE

Hodder & Stoughton
A MEMBER OF THE HODDER HEADLINE GROUP

British Library Cataloguing in Publication Data

Edmonds, John
 Business systems for leisure & tourism. – (Hodder GNVQ.
 Leisure & tourism in action)
 1. Tourist trade – Great Britain – Management 2. Leisure
 industry – Great Britain – Management
 I. Title
 338.4'791'068

ISBN 0 340 658398

First published 1997
Impression number   10 9 8 7 6 5 4 3 2 1
Year   2002 2001 2000 1999 1998 1997

Copyright © 1997 Sue Cundell

All rights reserved. No part of this publication may be reproduced or transmitted in any form or by any means, electronic or mechanical, including photocopy, recording or any information storage and retrieval system, without permission in writing from the publisher or under licence from the Copyright Licensing Agency Limited. Further details of such licences (for reprographic reproduction) may be obtained from the Copyright Licensing Agency limited, of 90 Tottenham Court Road, London W1P 9HE.

Typeset by Wearset, Boldon, Tyne and Wear.
Printed in Great Britain for Hodder & Stoughton Educational, a division of Hodder Headline Plc, 338 Euston Road, London NW1 3BH by Scotprint, Musselburgh, Scotland.

Contents

Acknowledgements	vi
Assessment matrix	vii
Introduction	ix

1 *Investigating and evaluating effectiveness of Administration systems in leisure and tourism organisations* ... 1
  Quality standards ... 1
  Administrative systems ... 4

2 *Communication systems in leisure and tourism organisations* ... 9
  Introduction ... 9
  Functions and purposes of communication systems ... 9
  Types of communication systems ... 10
  Electronic technology and communication ... 12
  The impact of electronic technology ... 13
  Evaluating the effectiveness of communication systems ... 14

3 *Information-processing systems in leisure and tourism industries* ... 16
  Introduction ... 16
  Functions of information-processing systems ... 17
  Purposes of information-processing systems ... 17
  Types of information-processing systems ... 19
  Main features of electronic technology used in information-processing systems ... 22
  Data Protection Act 1984 ... 23
  Evaluating the effectiveness of information-processing systems ... 24

4 *A visit to a Holiday World* ... 26
  Case study: Butlin's Southcoast World ... 26

5 *A visit to a theme park* ... 36
  Case study: LEGOLAND® ... 36

6 *Consultancy* ... 43
  Case study: Kirkham Hotel ... 43

Useful addresses ... 49
Glossary ... 50
Index ... 52

Acknowledgements

Appreciation is expressed to staff at Southcoast World and at LEGOLAND® who kindly gave up time to talk with with me about the operation of their organisation, and in particular about their business systems. Their assistance was invaluable. In particular I would like to thank: Southcoast World – Peter Keech, Graham Jones and Rodney Stinchcombe; LEGOLAND® Windsor – Rachel Townrow and Rob Baldry.

My thanks also to Philip Clarke and James Clarke for their advice relating to information technology.

The publishers would like to thank Life File for permission to reproduce copyright material (on pages 12 and 20).

Assessment Matrix

The tasks which appear in this volume have been devised to generate the Evidence Indicators of each Element of Unit 5: *Business Systems in the Leisure and Tourism Industries*, part of the Advanced GNVQ in Leisure and Tourism (1995 specifications). They will also meet the Performance Criteria (PCs) of the Key Skills Elements indicated below. The term 'Key Skills' is used instead of Core Skills throughout, and the Element numbers refer to 1995 specifications.

Students may provide evidence to meet grading criteria through each task. Task 14, which is the major summary assignment, involves complex activities and is most likely to generate evidence at Distinction level.

		Key Skills		
Task	Unit 5	Application of Number	Communication	Information Technology
1	5.1			
2	5.1			
3	5.1			
4	5.2			
5	5.2	3.3 pcs 2–4	3.3 pcs 1–2	3.3 pcs 1&4
6	5.2			
7	5.2			
8	5.3			
9	5.3		3.2 pcs 1–3	3.3 pcs 1&4
10	5.3			
11	5.3			3.4
12	5.3		3.2 pcs 1–5	
13	5.3			
14	5.1, 5.2, 5.3		3.2 pcs 1–5	3.4 pcs 1–4

Introduction to Business Systems in the Leisure and Tourism Industries

When you visit any leisure and tourism facility, such as a travel agent, sports centre, leisure complex or hotel, there is a great deal of routine work carried out which you, as the customer, do not see.

Business systems are in place to ensure that an organisation can meet your needs. If these vital 'behind the scenes' systems are efficient, they will be:

- contributing to any current success of the organisation and
- ensuring competitiveness

They will also form an important component in any future planning:

These business systems have been divided into three sub sets which will be looked at in turn in the following sections:

Section 1 **Administrative systems**
Section 2 **Communication systems**
Section 3 **Information-processing systems**

However, you need to be aware that these systems interlink and overlap.

The case studies in Section 4: Butlin's Southcoast World and Section 5: LEGOLAND® Windsor, will give an insight into business systems in specific leisure organisations.

Section 6 is a case study of an organisation that is in transition from a small family based business to a larger scale operation and you, with your new knowledge of business systems, will be asked to make recommendations for consideration by the owner. This report will cover all three systems.

As mentioned, business systems interlink and overlap. For example, a computer **reservation system** linked to a travel agency **Management Information System (MIS)** or accounting system is:

- an *administration* system keeping basic records of sales
- a *communication* system facilitating commu-

nication with the tour operator's **database** (and other databases) to identify holiday availability
- an *information-processing* system updating the tour operator's database and the travel agency's records and accounts when a booking is made.

The computer reservation system at Butlin's and the booking system at Legoland has similar functions. They are linked through a network with other computers on the site, and provide data on clients for the marketing and accounts departments, and give information which allows the organisation to plan ahead.

Any leisure and tourism organisation constantly reviews its business systems to ensure quality of products, services and facilities for you, the customer.

As you work through Sections 1, 2 and 3 there will be a number of tasks set which will ask you to consider specific aspects of business systems. A record of these considerations will aid you when it comes to writing the report on Kirkham Hotel, the case study in Section 6. You will therefore be keeping a 'notebook' in which you will record the outcome of the tasks set.

The evidence in your portfolio at the end of this unit will be:

- the report on the Kirkham Hotel
- the notebook recording the outcome of the tasks set.

The first time you meet a word or phrase which relates to aspects of business systems this will be highlighted and will be included in the glossary at the back of this book.

SECTION 1

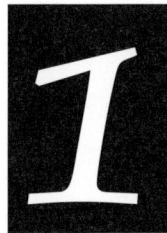

Investigating and Evaluating Effectiveness of Administration Systems in Leisure and Tourism Organisations

Key Aims

> In this section you will be examining the following aspects of administration systems in leisure and tourism organisations:
>
> - the main purpose of quality standards
> - the broad role of administration in the day-to-day running of a leisure or tourism organisation
> - the different administration systems which support the functions of leisure and tourism organisations.

QUALITY STANDARDS

Many leisure and tourism organisations have introduced, or are introducing, some kind of quality standard. This enables an organisation to monitor and evaluate aspects of its work against specific criteria and identify areas for improvement such as in the product, or in the services, they offer to customers.

An organisation can have quality standards for different aspects of its business, and at different levels. These quality standards could be:

- *internal* – set by the organisation. For example an hotel may have set the rule that the telephone will be answered within four rings, or in a restaurant a customer will have had his/her order dealt with within a specific time
- *external and voluntary* – the organisation could be looking to introduce **Investors in People (IIP)** which focuses on the training and development of staff, or **BS EN ISO 9000**, whose main focus is the consistent level of service or product delivery
- *external and compulsory* – such as the standards laid down in the Health and Safety at Work Act.

Not only are there different kinds of quality standards, there are different levels. These will include quality standards which are:

- *British* – mainly set by the **British Standards Institute (BSI)**. Sports facilities will need to ensure that any equipment they loan, such as protective headgear, meet these standards
- *European* – most are drawn up by the **European Commission (EC)** which issues directives detailing the requirements. An example is the Blue Flag criteria: if a seaside resort has been awarded the Blue Flag it tells a visitor that the resort has met the EC standards for beach and bathing water quality
- *International* – usually issued by different countries or groups of countries. They are mainly linked to the control of the quality of imports and exports. You will see products carrying the ISO mark which indicates that they have met the requirements of the **International Standards Organisation (ISO)**.

There is often confusion in the difference between **Quality Standards**, **Quality Assurance** and **Quality Control**.

- *Quality Standards* detail the level of quality which a product, service or facility provided for customers must meet
- *Quality Assurance* is the process of ensuring that a product, service or facility meets customer requirements. For example, a leisure complex will have quality standards laid down, sometimes set by themselves, sometimes by an outside body. Any members of staff responsible for quality assurance must ensure that these standards are being kept, so reducing the likelihood of any future problems
- *Quality Control* is the monitoring of the quality of the end product, service or facility to ensure that the standards are met. This may be done by inspecting the products such as food, or checking with customers to make sure that they are satisfied with the service they have received

We will consider three quality standards which are appropriate for the leisure and tourism industry in more detail:

- Investors in People
- BS EN ISO 9000
- **BS 7750 Environmental Management**

Investors in People (IIP)

The objective of this national quality standard, sponsored by the UK Government and administered by **Training and Enterprise Councils (TECs)**, is to improve business performance and secure competitive advantage. 'It sets a level of good practice for improving an organisation's performance through its people' (The Investors in People Standard 1996).

The result is a quality standard which provides a framework for action through:

- specifying the principles which tie training and development activity directly to business objectives
- ensuring resources committed to training and development are put to the most effective use
- providing a clear benchmark of good practice in training and development against which any organisation, large or small, can measure progress towards improved business performance.

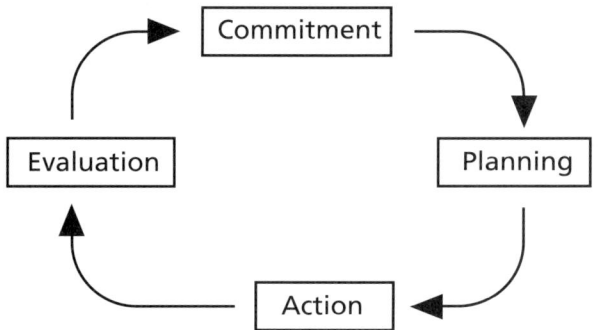

FIGURE 1.1 *Cyclical process based on the four key principles.*

It is stressed that the IIP Standard is about results – not procedures.

The IIP Quality Standard is based on four principles (see Figure 1.1), which reflect good training and development practice.

- *Commitment* – to develop all employees to achieve its business objective
- *Planning* – to regularly review the needs and plan the training and development of all employees
- *Action* – to take action to train and develop individuals on recruitment and throughout their employment
- *Evaluation* – to evaluate the investment in training and development to assess achievement and improve future effectiveness.

Any organisation which is an Investor in People must provide evidence that they meet all the criteria set down under each of the principles.

Figure 1.2 (see page 5) gives some of the advantages and disadvantages of implementing this standard, as does the case study relating to Southcoast World in Section 4.

BS EN ISO 9000

This is an international standard which acts as a framework to allow an organisation to develop a quality system to suit its own way of working.

It lays down a general set of principles about management practice and operational procedures:

- under management practice will be the specification of criteria and procedures to ensure that products and services meet customers' requirements such as document control, quality systems to be in place, audits, training
- under operational procedures are criteria for measuring the consistency of an organisation's systems such as:
  - dealing with orders from customers
  - purchasing of stock and stock control
  - handling, storage, packaging, preservation and delivery
  - quality records
  - providing a service to customers.

There are three major alternative parts to the standards, and an organisation will choose the one which is most appropriate for them.

BS 7750 Environmental Management

Although this award is currently national, it will form the basis of an international ISO 14000 series of environmental standards.

There has been growing concern over the impact an organisation has on the environment, both the local environment of the organisation, and wider. For example, tour operators based in Britain can, and do, have an impact in the countries to which they send their clients. Legoland worked closely with local community groups when it developed the theme park at Windsor.

If an organisation decides to adopt the standard, then central to that organisation must be a commitment to control its environmental performance. The standard provides a management tool for these organisations.

When an organisation has decided it will introduce a quality standard it usually sets up a review of its current position, whether in terms of administrative systems, training of staff, impact on an environment, or procedures for purchasing stock. This will give the organisation a **baseline** against which they can measure future improvement against the standards – whether internally or externally set.

Targets will then be set for the organisation. When an organisation is going for a national or international award, an external assessor will be involved in the initial review and in assessing any developments towards meeting the standards. They will confirm when the quality standard has been met so that the award can be made. The organisation can then use the quality standard logo; you can see these on company letterheads and in publicity material. After a few years the organisation will be re-assessed to ensure that it is still meeting the standard.

Therefore, by implementing a quality standard, the organisation will:

- identify the current position
- identify where improvements need to be made
- ensure that all procedures are fully documented and audited to assure and control the quality of the product, or service, for the customer.

All three of the above quality standards are relevant to leisure and tourism, and relevant to business systems.

The comments opposite reflect the views of staff in leisure and tourism organisations who have been involved in the implementation of a quality standard.

TASK 1

In your notebook:

1 Summarise the reasons why an organisation should introduce a quality standard.
2 Against each of the three quality standards:

Investors in People
BS EN ISO 9000
BS 7750

identify:

(i) why a leisure and tourism industry might wish to introduce that specific quality standard, and the benefits of this, particularly in terms of business systems
(ii) any disadvantages that have to be borne in mind.

There are further details of reasons, advantages and disadvantages in Figure 1.2 and in the case studies in Sections 4 and 5.

ADMINISTRATIVE SYSTEMS

Why we need administrative systems

There are **routine functions** and **non-routine functions** in any leisure and tourism organisation.

- *Routine functions* are the day-to-day functions such as:
  - dealing with customer enquiries
  - handling and recording cash
  - stock control
  - cleaning and maintenance
- *Non-routine functions* include:
  - producing occasional information
  - dealing with accidents or emergencies

Systems will need to be in place to support these functions. There needs to be:

- clear procedures laid down for staff to fol-

INVESTIGATING AND EVALUATING EFFECTIVENESS OF ADMINISTRATION SYSTEMS

IIP

'It has allowed us to review our current training and development against a good practice benchmark, and so we have an accurate picture of current strengths and weaknesses.'

'Not all staff wished to take part in any training activity.'

'As a manager I find IIP provides a framework for planning future strategy and action.'

'The cost of the training was very expensive; I think we will look to develop more in-house trainers in the future.'

• • • • • • •

ISO 9000

'I'm glad we finally went for the award. We now have consistency in the way we respond to customers.'

'A lot of staff resent having to follow all the procedures which they sometimes see as being too bureaucratic and paper led – it takes too much time to complete.'

'There is greater clarity in job roles. All staff now have a clear job description which tells them what they have to do and how.'

'The ISO 9000 logo looks good on the headed notepaper. Customers seem to like this – it gives them confidence in what we produce.'

• • • • • • •

BS 7750 Environmental Management

'By going for this award it has shown to our customers that we give priority to our commitment to take action which will reduce damage to the environment.'

'We have closely examined all our processes, and the raw materials we buy. In some instances we have saved money, and in others it has led to improved productivity.'

'Not all staff have seen the need to change, and have been sceptical of any initiatives that have been introduced.'

'Some benefits have been rather slow, and costs have been higher than expected.'

FIGURE 1.2 *Advantages and disadvantages of implementing quality standards.*

low such as when making reservations for accommodation; when accepting cash or cheques from customers
- records kept of transactions such as customer enquiries; reservations made; money taken; stock ordered
- summaries made, i.e. a sports centre manager may wish to see an overview of the bookings of a specific facility such as the squash courts, and summaries of payments into, and from, an organisation.

Efficient and effective administrative systems are necessary:

- for the smooth running of an organisation
- to enable an organisation to identify and measure whether it is meeting its objectives – financial or otherwise
- to ensure that financial, human and physical resources are used to best effect
- to meet customer expectations – efficient systems impress customers
- to comply with relevant legislation such as health and safety, employment of staff
- to monitor the effectiveness and efficiency of the organisation.

Examples of administrative systems

Figure 1.3 identifies some of the administrative activities for which a system will be in place relating to financial, human and physical resources.

In addition, there will be administrative activity in the areas of:

- customer service, such as collecting customers' opinions, after-sales service
- quality assurance: monitoring the process and the end product or service. This will be particularly relevant for organisations who have introduced a quality standard.

Some of these areas overlap. A training manager in a company with dedicated training rooms, such as in Southcoast World in Section 4, would use administrative systems from all three resources.

- *Financial* – sending out invoices, paying bills
- *Physical* – maintaining a training environment
- *Human* – training staff in customer relations.

Although some administrative systems are still paper based, most are now computer based.

Evaluating administrative systems

Having set up administrative systems, an organisation needs to evaluate these regularly in terms of:

Type of Resource	Administrative activities and systems
Financial	Sending out invoices Paying bills Recording sales Handling payments, including cash
Physical	Maintenance of environment Health and Safety
Human	Staff recruitment Staff training Staff appraisal Disciplinary procedures

FIGURE 1.3 *Resources and administrative systems.*

INVESTIGATING AND EVALUATING EFFECTIVENESS OF ADMINISTRATION SYSTEMS

TASK 2

In your notebook identify:

1. A specific leisure and tourism organisation such as a sports complex, hotel, travel agent, cinema, etc. and then identify:

   (i) four examples of administrative systems which support routine functions
   (ii) one example of a system which supports a non-routine function

   Draw upon the case studies, and upon your personal knowledge through your own visits as a customer, or on work experience.

2. Make brief notes, possibly under bullet points, about why you feel it is important that these systems have been set up.

- Fitness for purpose
- Value for money
- Accuracy
- Efficiency
- Security
- Ease of use
- User opinion

This will ensure that a system is still effective and meets the needs of the organisation, and of customers.

Fitness for purpose
Does the system do what it is supposed to do? If there has been a new booking system for accommodation set up, does this show up-to-date information on which accommodation is booked and by whom, and which accommodation is available?

Value for money
Is the system cost effective? For example, if the organisation has spent a great deal of money purchasing a computerised system, has the expense been worthwhile – has it saved time and money previously spent on paper-based systems?

Accuracy
Is the information generated by the system accurate and reliable? Very precise details will be needed by a travel agent to ensure that two different families are not booked into the same hotel room, or that two people have not been booked on the same seat in an aeroplane.

Efficiency
Does the system work with minimum waste of time and effort? If it is a computerised system with information that is needed by a number of different people, can this be accessed easily? If it is a paper system, such as a wall planner relating to holiday leave, is it accessible and easy to understand?

Security
How secure is the information stored either on a computer, or in a paper-based system? Is confidential or sensitive information stored securely and access restricted?

Ease of use
Can staff use the system easily? At Southcoast World they chose a specific system particularly because it was easy for staff to use, and this minimised the need for extensive training. Staff felt confident in using it. As it was easier to use, the information put into the system tended to be more accurate.

User opinion
Are those using the system happy and confident with it? Are their views and suggestions listened to?

TASK 3

You work for a consultancy firm which has been asked to evaluate the business systems used by an hotel. Part of the evaluation will be of the administrative systems they have in place.

Your manager has asked you to draw up a list of questions to check how well the administrative system is working at this hotel.

Draw up these questions in your notebook under the following headings:

- Fitness for purpose
- Value for money
- Accuracy
- Efficiency
- Security
- Ease of use
- User opinion

SECTION 2

Communication Systems in Leisure and Tourism Organisations

Key Aims

In this section you will be examining the following aspect of communication systems in leisure and tourism organisations:

- functions and purposes of communications systems
- types of communications systems
- how the development of electronic technology has affected communications systems.

INTRODUCTION

Effective communication is an essential component of a successful organisation, particularly in the leisure and tourism industry. With the strong emphasis on people, staff working in a leisure and tourism organisation need to be good communicators as this is likely to be a large part of their job – communicating with customers, colleagues, and outside organisations such as suppliers. They will use different types of communication such as face-to-face, telephone, **e-mail**, signs, posters, leaflets.

FUNCTIONS AND PURPOSES OF COMMUNICATION SYSTEMS

Communication systems have a number of functions:

- to support the management and operation

of the organisation. There needs to be a flow of information within an organisation. Good communication of accurate information and data will aid decision makers to make sound judgements and to monitor the smooth running and performance of the organisation
- to facilitate links with external organisations, such as the Inland Revenue when information is needed relating to accounts, and emergency services such as fire and police
- to facilitate links with individuals such as customers, and the general public.

The purpose of these communication systems is to provide internal and external channels for exchanging information.

- **Internal communication channels**. At Legoland advance booking figures are passed from the admissions section to the restaurants on site so they can order sufficient fresh food. In an organisation information will also be passed from personnel to the wages department, and data will be gathered for the annual accounts
- **External communication channels**. These communication links will be with organisations and with individuals: travel agents need to reserve airline seats; catering supplies need to be ordered by hotels; confirmation of bookings are sent to customers; complaints by individuals need to be responded to.

TYPES OF COMMUNICATION SYSTEMS

The main types of communication are verbal, written and electronic, although there is an overlap as e-mail is written and electronic. Some types of communication will be predominantly for internal communication such as memos, meetings and noticeboards. Examples of types of external communication include marketing leaflets, and letters to customers and suppliers. As expected, many types of communication are used for both internal and external communication such as telephone conversations and e-mail.

Communication can be one-way or two-way.

One-way communication systems

One-way communication is when information is given in one direction only, with no immediate response from the receiver of the message. Examples of one-way communication can be seen in Figure 2.1

As information is given in one direction only there will be:

- a sender
- a chosen method of sending the message
- a receiver of the message.

As there is no immediate response to the message given, there needs to be additional care

---

◊ Signs, signposts, notices, interpretation panels, display panels
◊ Written correspondence: letters, memos, fax
◊ Public address systems
◊ Guided tours on cassette
◊ Leaflets: marketing leaflets, information leaflets
◊ Items on radio and television
◊ Pages on the Internet
◊ Computer-generated speech

FIGURE 2.1 *Examples of one-way communication systems.*

COMMUNICATION SYSTEMS IN LEISURE AND TOURISM ORGANISATIONS

> ◊ Face-to-face conversations
> ◊ Meetings
> ◊ Telephone conversations
> ◊ Intercom systems
> ◊ Mobile radio
> ◊ **Video conferencing**
> ◊ Interactive computer programmes
> ◊ Sign language

FIGURE 2.2 *Examples of two-way communication systems.*

in deciding layout and wording so that the receiver does not misinterpret the message.

Two-way communication systems

In two-way communication there is communication in both directions: there is both sending and receiving of a message, with interaction between sender and receiver. You can see examples of two-way communication systems in Figure 2.2.

As there is communication in both directions there will be:

- the sender
- the method of sending the message
- the receiver of the message
- the response to the message back to the sender.

Unlike one-way communication, in two-way communication the receiver can immediately clarify any misunderstandings or confusions. Remember that communication is not always in spoken or written form. Non-verbal communication through our body language is important and can reinforce what we are saying. It can also contradict what we may be saying. For example, we may be assuring a customer that we have plenty of time to deal with their enquiry and we are interested in what they are saying, but our body language may be indicating that we are not interested as we avoid eye contact, keep looking towards other people and 'drum' our fingers on the table.

It is also important to remember that the image of the company is reflected in the quality of the communication we use. For example, letters are probably the most commonly used type of external written communication. The presentation and content gives the receiver an image of the organisation, and if the layout on the page is poor and there are spelling and grammatical mistakes, the receiver will form a bad impression and might decide not to use the organisation because of this. At both Southcoast World and Legoland there is a handbook for staff which gives the official company format for the layout of letters, and this reinforces the company image.

When there is verbal two-way communication via the telephone, both parties should speak clearly and concisely – time can be money as long-distance calls may be expensive.

BUSINESS SYSTEMS FOR LEISURE AND TOURISM

TASK 4

1 Select:
   (i) two examples of the types of one-way communication systems given in Figure 2.1
   (ii) two examples of the types of two-way communication systems given in Figure 2.2

2 In your notebook identify:
   (i) the main advantages and
   (ii) the potential problems
   with each of the four types of communication systems.

TASK 5

During conversations you discover that you and your friends spend your leisure hours in an average week as follows:

Watching television	6.2 hrs
Going to a disco	3.0 hrs
At a sports centre	4.3 hrs
Going to the cinema	2.5 hrs
Going to a music club or concert	1.5 hrs

You decide to send this information to your school/college newspaper, and need to communicate this information in a more interesting way, such as a graph, chart, etc.

Using information technology, produce a visual presentation of this information which will be appropriate for the readers of the newspaper.

ELECTRONIC TECHNOLOGY AND COMMUNICATION

The rapid rise in the development and use of electronic technology in the leisure and tourism industry has affected communication systems. Electronic communication systems are being used more frequently as an alternative to paper-based systems. Many organisations have introduced computer systems and electronic equipment to improve internal and external communication.

Electronic communication methods include the following.

- **Computer reservation systems**. In both case studies in this book the organisations have developed a database which contains information about availability of tickets or accommodation, customer details, etc.
- **Computer networks**. This is when computers have been networked, or linked to each other. Staff can then access other computers, or one central computer, within the same network. It is possible for information to be centrally stored, such as advanced booking figures, so that other users can access this information
- **Electronic mail (e-mail).** A computer-based system which allows the transmission of information directly from one registered e-mail user to another

COMMUNICATION SYSTEMS IN LEISURE AND TOURISM ORGANISATIONS

- **Enhanced telephone systems** such as:
  - **fax** which allows for the transmission of information and documents via a telephone line
  - **modems** which enable computers to speak to each other using a telephone link although they may be in different places
  - **Internet** which is sometimes called the 'information highway', 'the net' or 'the web'. Computer users can access information on databases. Organisations can have their own pages on 'the net' with information (such as marketing information) which others on 'the net' can access
- **Voice comprehension and generation**. This is when technology can understand simple oral messages and can create a simple and appropriate answer. An example of voice comprehension is when you make a telephone call and a recorded voice at the other end asks you a question. Your voice response gives you access to further information – possibly train times or cinema details
- **Touch screens**. Staff can use and control a computer by touching a screen rather than using a keyboard or mouse. Staff at ticket offices use them, and some have been installed in museums. If customers want information on a particular exhibit they can just touch a picture on a screen and the computer will generate the information for them to see

You may find further forms of telecommunication in an organisation such as automatic answering machines, mobile telephones, electronic paging devices, call transfer facilities, freephone telephone systems – all of which support and aid communication internally and externally.

THE IMPACT OF ELECTRONIC TECHNOLOGY

Electronic technology has affected both the organisation, and the individuals within the organisation.

Impact on the organisation

Staff who work at Southcoast World and Legoland spoke of the impact electronic technology had had. They, and other organisations, have commented on:

- the increase in *speed* of communications. For example, the fax allows fast and accurate sending of copies of documents, or the confirmation of a booking; e-mail enables accurate and immediate transmission of information directly from one computer to another, or from one sender to a group of receivers
- *accuracy*, such as in the transmission of documents either through fax or e-mail, and the production of accurate booking details sent to customers. This does, however, rely on accurate input of information by staff
- *reliability* – not only will there be reliable information which can be accessed, such as in computerised reservations systems, but answering machines and fax machines do not take sick leave nor holidays
- *productivity* – you can leave messages on e-mail rather than waiting for someone to answer the telephone; an answering machine can take messages when you are out, or busy; bookings can be taken more speedily for the customer on a computerised booking system
- *costs* – savings can be made if there is an increase in productivity. If staff are not tied up on the telephone, productivity is improved. One co-ordinated single computer reservation system which has replaced several more time consuming paper-based systems can reduce costs and increase productivity
- *access to information* – the computer reserva-

tion system allows computer users, particularly if part of a computer network, to access information.

Impact on the individual

When electronic technology is introduced into a company there is a need for staff to learn how to use, and feel comfortable with, the new system. If they do not use the technology accurately this will in turn hinder effective communication.

Staff also have access to information which previously may not have been available. For example, they can make decisions based on more accurate data and they will have information more readily available to answer customers' queries.

TASK 6

1. Select two electronic communications systems.
2. Identify the likely impact on an organisation and the individual within that organisation for both of these systems.

EVALUATING THE EFFECTIVENESS OF COMMUNICATIONS SYSTEMS

When evaluating the effectiveness of a communication system you need to use the same criteria as when you evaluated the administrative systems, and you may wish to refer back to Section 1:

- Fitness for purpose
- Value for money
- Accuracy
- Efficiency
- Security
- Ease of use
- User opinion

Fitness for purpose
If a new communication system is purchased or developed because there was a need to improve internal communications, has the system done this? Is there improved communication? Do staff have access to more information? Is communication faster?

Value for money
Is the system cost-effective? Have savings been made in terms of staff time through its introduction?

Accuracy
Is the information and data transmitted through the system accurate and reliable? Can the receiver of a fax read the message clearly?

Efficiency
Is there more efficient use of staff time? If a computer-based system is being evaluated, how reliable is it? Does it frequently break down and cause communication problems?

Security
Are there restrictions on who can access specific information? For example, it would not be appropriate for all staff to access confidential personnel information.

Ease of use
Do those who use the communication system, whether paper based or electronic based, find it easy to use and understand?

User opinion
What do those who use the communication think of it? If it is paper based, is it too cumbersome? Are there too many forms? If it is electronic based, is there too much to learn?

COMMUNICATION SYSTEMS IN LEISURE AND TOURISM ORGANISATIONS

TASK 7

1 List six examples of communication systems you have met in your contact with leisure and tourism organisations, both one-way and two-way. You may have been to a bowling alley, skating rink, cinema, theme park, travel agent or sports match. You may have called a cinema to enquire about a film, or a football club to book a ticket.

2 From the six examples, choose one one-way communication system and one two-way communication system.

3 For each of these two communication systems, evaluate the effectiveness of the communication in terms of:
- fitness for purpose
- value for money
- accuracy
- efficiency
- security
- ease of use
- user opinion

Although you were the receiver of the message, when evaluating the communication also consider the communication system from the point of view of the sender.

SECTION 3

Information-processing Systems in Leisure and Tourism Industries

Key Aims

In this section you will be examining the following aspects of information-processing systems in leisure and tourism organisations:

- functions and purposes of information-processing systems
- types of information-processing systems
- the main features of electronic technology used in information-processing systems
- the effects of the Data Protection Act 1984 on users and operators of information-processing systems.

INTRODUCTION

Access to information is crucial in leisure and tourism organisations. For example, information is needed by management so that decisions can be accurate and up-to-date, and customers' expectations that their requests for information are answered speedily can be met.

The rise in the use of electronic technology in leisure and tourism organisations has meant that tasks which were once manual have now been automated. Staff therefore need training in the new technology.

FUNCTIONS OF INFORMATION-PROCESSING SYSTEMS

All organisations need to be able to process information about themselves and their customers.

The case study organisations – Southcoast World and Legoland – process information about:

- their organisation, such as staff wages, staff training, accounts, use of different facilities on the site and admission levels
- customers, such as bookings and mailing lists for marketing special offers

An organisation may use a manual or electronic information-processing system. However, the main functions are still the same:

- Receiving information
- Storing information
- Distributing information

Some sophisticated computer-based programmes are also able to *analyse information*.

PURPOSES OF INFORMATION-PROCESSING SYSTEMS

An organisation needs to provide information relating to customer service and relating to management. Different leisure and tourism organisations will have different information needs. The information needed by the manager of a small guest house will be very different to that needed by the manager of a large leisure complex.

Providing customer service information

When an organisation is providing customer service information, it is providing information to someone else outside. Staff in the organisation are responding to external enquirers, and examples of this service include:

- a travel agent providing information about different resorts and the availability of accommodation in these resorts
- a bus, or railway, station providing travel timetables
- a tourist information centre providing information about the locality such as beauty spots or recreational centres. They may also be asked about the availability of bed and breakfast accommodation in the area
- a cinema providing details of the films for the coming week, including the times of showing. Customers may wish to know if there are any seats available at specific showings
- a football club providing details of home and away matches, ticket availability and cost.

An organisation may keep details of the number and type of enquiries they have had about a particular product or service as this information can be of use for future planning.

Providing management information

People who run a leisure and tourism organisation need information to be provided so they can make effective decisions. This information could relate to financial data, operations such as stock control, occupancy of accommodation and about customers.

Many organisations are implementing a **management information system** which is a mix of both manual and automated systems, although more usually now computer-based, which enables the collection, collation, storage, retrieval, analysis and use of data to support the management and forward planning of an organisation. Figure 3.1 on page 18 shows an analysis of information depicted as a graph.

There is a need to provide certain information for **statutory** purposes. A company must:

- publish its annual accounts and
- present its **VAT** records

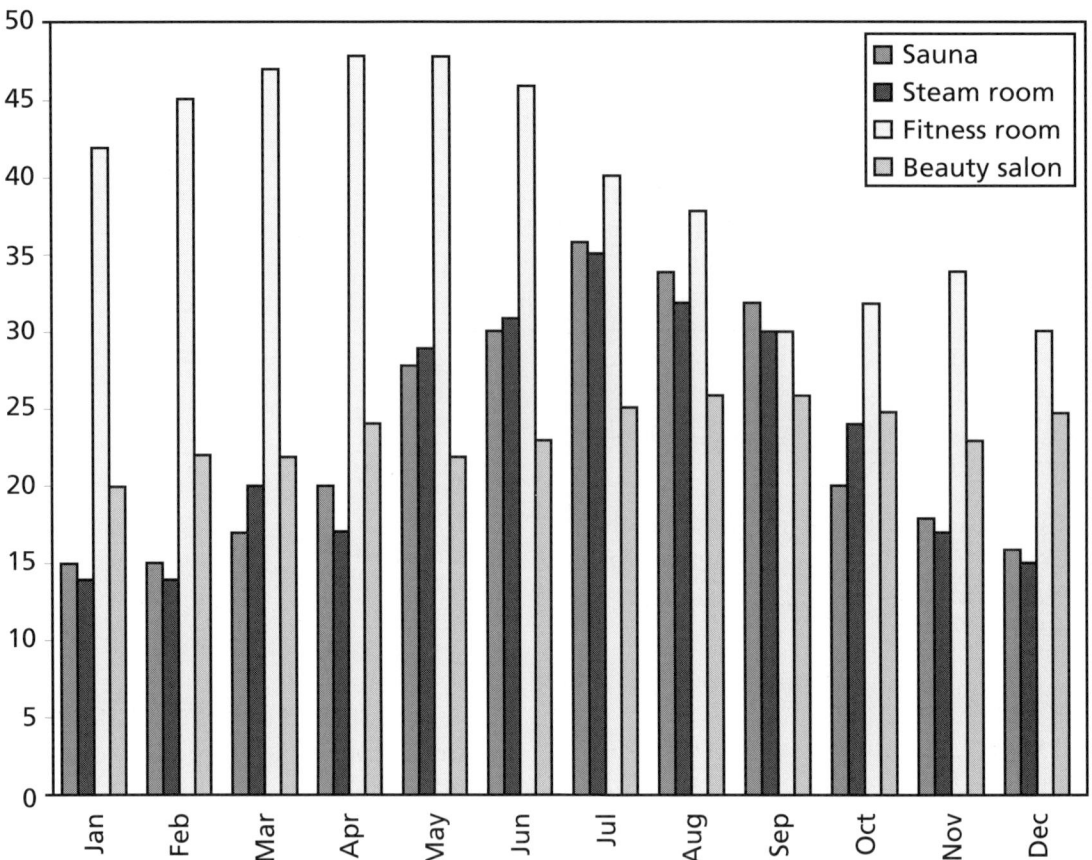

FIGURE 3.1 *Analysis of information relating to the use of facilities at a health club.*

and data will need to be gathered, stored and retrieved for these purposes.

There is information which management needs to control the operation of the organisation. This information could include:

- daily summaries, such as visitors to a wildlife park
- monthly statistics, such as sales figures from a shop in a leisure centre
- annual analyses – a theme park may wish to look at which of its rides has been used most by children, and which has been used least; a manager of a hotel may want information relating to use of the hotel restaurant by both guests staying in the hotel and outside visitors to the hotel.

TASK 8

Draw up a checklist of the type of information which would be needed by a manager of a small hotel. The hotel has 20 rooms, and employs 3 full-time, and 4 part-time staff.

Organisations have front-office activities and back-office activities. As customers, you tend to have face-to-face contact with staff who are involved in front-office activities. In some organisations these activities may also be called front-of-house. Figure 3.2 gives examples of front-office activities and Figure 3.3 gives examples of back-office activities in the two case study organisations.

INFORMATION-PROCESSING SYSTEMS IN LEISURE AND TOURISM INDUSTRIES

> ◊ Welcoming visitors
> ◊ Providing information
> ◊ Answering queries
> ◊ Bookings
> ◊ Ticket sales
> ◊ Controlling entry
> ◊ Handling cash, cheques, credit and debit cards
> ◊ Promoting services and products
> ◊ Passing information to different sections in the 'back office'

FIGURE 3.2 *Examples of front-office activities at Southcoast World and Legoland.*

> ◊ Accounting
> ◊ Stock control
> ◊ Staff training
> ◊ Analysis of data for management, marketing, accounts
> ◊ Health and safety
> ◊ Financial dealings – cash, credit, banking

FIGURE 3.3 *Examples of back-office activities at Southcoast World and Legoland.*

TASK 9

Consider a small hotel with a restaurant. Which administrative and information processing activities are likely to be front-office and which back-office.

Present this information in two columns under a main heading. In one column give examples of front office activities and in the second column, back office activities. If you have access to a computer, draw up the table using one of the software programmes.

TYPES OF INFORMATION-PROCESSING SYSTEMS

Most organisations use both manual and electronic systems for processing information.

Manual information-processing systems

A manual task is something done by hand – not done mechanically or by computer. In a number of organisations a manual information processing system to meet the needs and purposes of the organisation will still be the most cost effective and appropriate system to use. They may be faster than electronic ones, easier to use, and easier to access.

Manual information-processing systems include the following.

- **Booking forms.** The manager of a small guest house may find it much faster and easier to write the details of a customer directly onto a booking form. Others working in the same organisation can quickly look

at the relevant page to see if there are any vacancies on a specific day (see Figure 3.6)
- **Paper filing systems.** In some organisations, staff who need access to information might not have a computer, and so certain information is stored centrally in a filing cabinet (see Figure 3.4)

FIGURE 3.4 *Multiplication – the number of filing cabinets can increase as the amount of paper increases.*

- **Card indexes.** These could include information relating to suppliers, customers, staff (see Figure 3.5)
- **Charts.** The visual information contained in a wall chart giving details of duty rosters, or holidays, can be easier to use and easier to access. It enables management to see when additional staff may needed to cover for those on leave
- **Cash books and ledgers.** If it is a small organisation with very few transactions being made, it may be cheaper to continue with the system of entering details into cash books and ledgers than invest a great deal of money in a computer system which could become obsolete, and which will require investment in staff training.

Electronic information-processing systems

An electronic information-processing system is usually controlled by a computer. Computers have both hardware and software.

Hardware: the physical computer equipment, such as:

- *VDU (visual display unit)* which displays the data on a monochrome or colour screen
- *keyboard* which is used to input data into the computer
- *mouse* (manually operated user signal encoder) which is also used to input data
- *scanner* which can copy text, graphics or photographs into the computer memory
- *printer* which prints out the hard copy.

INFORMATION-PROCESSING SYSTEMS IN LEISURE AND TOURISM INDUSTRIES

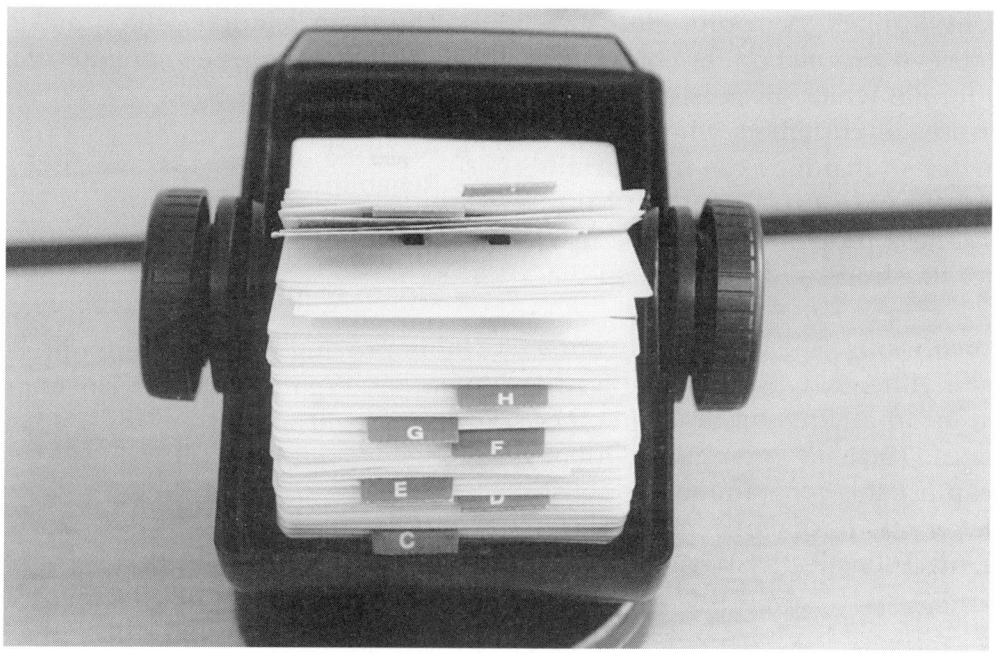

FIGURE 3.5 *Address card system which enables easy access by staff.*

Software: the computer programmes, or applications, which enable the users to perform functions such as the following.

- *Wordprocessing.* This programme allows the user to input text to produce letters, minutes of meetings, reports, memos, tables of figures. It has replaced the typewriter in many offices. Some word processing programmes have features such as mail-merge, spell-checking, simple graphics

- *Spreadsheets.* Numbers are processed and presented in a standard format which is usually rows and columns. They enable users to make fast calculations and financial projections. Graphs and tables can be produced directly from the information held on the database, such as in Figure 3.1

- *Databases.* Information such as names and addresses of customers, members and suppliers, can be stored on databases. The programme can also sort data and present this

Burton Photographic Club Date:									
Facility	Time								
	9–10 am	10–11 am	11–12 am	12–1 pm	1–2 pm	2–3 pm	3–4 pm	4–5 pm	5–6 pm
Studio 1									
Studio 2									
Dark room									

FIGURE 3.6 *Example of a paper-based form enabling the booking of facilities by photographic club members. When a member books a studio, or the dark room, their name is entered in the appropriate square.*

in different formats. A sports club may wish to retrieve information from the database in a format which gives all the names and addresses of customers who are aged 16 and under so that they can mail details of a special offer to them
- *Graphics.* These programmes can be used to produce illustrations, drawings and diagrams
- *Desktop publishing.* The user can lay out a document in different ways, using different fonts, and incorporating images from other programmes such as graphics. Organisations can use this programme to publish a newsletter, a business report, travel brochure, marketing leaflet, posters.

MAIN FEATURES OF ELECTRONIC TECHNOLOGY USED IN INFORMATION-PROCESSING SYSTEMS

Organisations can spend a great deal of money on information technology, but not always wisely. Thought has to be given to why it is needed, and the implications for customers and staff. The reasons for purchasing and installing a particular computer system will vary between different organisations.

The main features which make electronic technology attractive to organisations are:
- Speed
- Accuracy
- Reliability
- Costs
- Productivity
- Access to information

By improving an information-processing system, an organisation is also improving the service to customers.

Speed

A computer system can speed up the processing of information, and of making complex calculations. Customers making bookings can be dealt with more efficiently, and confirmation letters sent out immediately.

Accuracy

If the information which has been fed into a computer is accurate then the information produced will also be accurate. The most frequent errors are human errors linked to inputting data. However, faults in computer hardware and software also cause errors. For example, some new software packages (par-

---

TASK 10

Think back to the last two or three occasions when you visited or telephoned a leisure and tourism organisation to obtain information. This may have been a visit to a travel agent to ask about a holiday, a sports centre to ask about the availability of a squash court, or a sports club to ask if any tickets were left for a particular game/match.

Make a note on:

(i) the information you were seeking on these occasions
(ii) The records which would have been consulted by staff to get that information.

Identify two manual information-processing systems and two electronic information-processing systems they may have used.

ticularly those used for spreadsheets) have had in-built faults which were only discovered through using the programme.

Reliability

Computers have become more reliable, although occasionally they may 'crash'. This is why Southcoast World and Legoland have systems in place to ensure that should a fault occur, or there is a power cut, a back-up system exists for saving any information which has been inputted.

Both organisations employ information technology specialists to support staff and deal with any problems.

Costs

Although the initial cost of installing a computer system can be high, savings can be made with increased productivity, and a possible reduction of staffing levels.

Productivity

The introduction of a computer system may not necessarily mean a reduction in staff, but will enable the same number of staff to do much more. Highly skilled staff need not spend so much time on everyday administrative functions, and can be involved in more complex duties.

Access to information

A great deal of information can be stored on, and dealt with, by a computer. People within, and external to, the organisation have access to more information. A leisure and tourism organisation may also gain access to data from other organisations. There are direct computer links between Southcoast World and some travel agents, so bookings can be made easily.

TASK 11

The manager of a club you belong to (or know about) is wondering whether or not to get a computer for the office as they are dealing with a great deal of information. S/he would like to discuss this with you.

Ahead of this meeting, identify the main features of electronic technology used in information-processing systems which could influence the decision of the manager. You need to consider what types of information the club may be dealing with, and whether/how electronic technology will be appropriate.

DATA PROTECTION ACT 1984

This Act gave the individual the right to access information held in computer databases containing personal information, and the right to have such information held securely.

The Act does not apply to information stored on a manual system such as in paper files, index cards.

An individual has the right to know what computerised records are held about them by an organisation and to correct any information that is incorrect.

Any organisation which stores personal data on a computer is required to comply with the Act, and must register with the Data Protection Register.

The aim of the Act is to regulate the way in which data is gathered, stored and disclosed to third parties, and to 'restrict living individuals being harmed by the abuse of personal information or data'.

Staff must ensure that:

- the information held on the computer has been obtained fairly, and the provider was not misled about the purpose for which the information was being obtained

- the personal information about individuals is secure
- there is restricted access to the information
- personal data should be accurate, updated as and when necessary, and relevant to the purpose disclosed to the Data Protection Registry. This information should not be kept longer than is necessary.

EVALUATING THE EFFECTIVENESS OF INFORMATION-PROCESSING SYSTEMS

As in Sections 1 and 2, consideration needs to be given to the following when evaluating the effectiveness of an information-processing system:

- Fitness for purpose
- Value for money
- Accuracy
- Efficiency
- Security
- Ease of use
- User opinion

Fitness for purpose
An organisation needs to have clearly defined what it wants from an information-processing system to meet the objectives of the company.

Value for money
Has too much money been spent on an information-processing system? – there are many systems available. Does it provide value for money – an organisation may need specialist advice as to which is most cost-effective.

Accuracy
Most errors are human errors. Are many errors occurring? Are these human errors, or software/hardware problems?

Efficiency
Are people's jobs easier? Has the service to customers improved? Has the information produced improved the management of the organisation?

Security
Does the company abide by the requirements of the Data Protection Act? Is there restricted access to confidential information?

Ease of use
Is the system easy to use, and understand? Is there support and training available for those who need it?

User opinion
Formal and informal feedback is useful from staff, customers and managers. Is the system, whether manual or electronic, meeting their needs?

TASK 12

Consider two information-processing systems which may be in your school/college/local library, one manual and one electronic.

For both systems, identify what you would look at when evaluating each system.

Consider these issues:

- fitness for purpose
- value for money
- accuracy
- efficiency
- security
- ease of use
- user opinion.

INFORMATION-PROCESSING SYSTEMS IN LEISURE AND TOURISM INDUSTRIES

TASK 13

A member of your team was going to visit Westham Leisure Centre to find out about their information-processing system but has been taken ill. The appointment cannot be re-arranged. Ideally you – Chris Brown – would have gone in their place, but you are not available at that time. Another colleague, Alex Frost, is going instead.

The following is the content of a memo you receive from Alex Frost:

WEST CONSULTANCY

MEMO

From: Alex Frost
To: Chris Brown

As you know I am visiting the Westham Leisure Centre to discuss their information-processing systems. I would be grateful if you could send me brief notes on:

(A) the main features of electronic technology used in information-processing systems

(B) the effects of the Data Protection Act on users and operators

There is some urgency, so could you please let me have details by the end of the week.

Please reply to this memo.

SECTION

A Visit to a Holiday World

CASE STUDY: BUTLIN'S SOUTHCOAST WORLD

Key Aims

> In this section you will be examining a case study of a leisure provision and looking at the business systems they operate in order to meet the needs of their customers. You will consider:
>
> - the structure of the organisation
> - the business systems they operate in order to meet the needs of their customers
> - the external quality systems
> - how staff training needs are met.

INTRODUCTION

Billy Butlin opened his first holiday camp at Skegness in 1936. In Britain there are now five Butlin's Leisure Worlds.

- Somerwest World, Minehead, Somerset
- Southcoast World, Bognor Regis, West Sussex
- Funcoast World, Skegness, Lincolnshire
- Starcoast World, Pwllheli, North Wales
- Wonderwest World, Ayr, Scotland

In addition there are five Holiday Hotels at Margate, Brighton, Scarborough, Blackpool, Llandudno, and The Grand Hotel in London.

Southcoast World is a leisure world on a 60-

A VISIT TO A HOLIDAY WORLD

FIGURE 4.1 *All business systems seek to ensure that visitors enjoy their stay at Southcoast World.*

acre site which is almost the size of a small town. Although there is clear signposting, visitors are given a map on their arrival.

At peak holiday times Southcoast World can accommodate up to 5,000 residential customers and also welcomes 5,500 day visitors.

They employ approximately 1,300 staff to ensure that customers' needs are met.

At Southcoast World, as is the case in a great many of the other Leisure Worlds, visitors have a choice of accommodation (as in Figure 4.2), and through the booking system will select a range of **full-board**, **half-board**,

FIGURE 4.2 *Accommodation: reservations systems need to ensure that customers who reserve premier accommodation can be assured of this on their arrival.*

self-catering or a mixture. Within this range there is also a choice of accommodation ranging from 'budget' through to luxury or 'premier' accommodation.

At Southcoast World holiday-makers have access to:

- sports facilities
- entertainment for all ages during the day and evening
- restaurants
- bars
- shops
- cinemas

Each of the Holiday Worlds are autonomous profit-making businesses within the larger parent company.

The organisational structure of Southcoast World can be seen in Figure 4.3 where the operations have been grouped into main functions: Personnel and Training, Leisure Services, Customer Services, Food and Beverage, Shops and Finance.

Each of the functions is headed up by an Executive Manager who reports to the Centre Director who oversees the profitability and the delivery of the product across the whole of the business. Although it is a powerful management team, there is still flexibility and autonomy, and any changes that are introduced are within clearly defined guidelines.

It is important for such a large company as Butlin's to have a unified front so customers will recognise their style, their name, their logo. For example, there is a corporate identity manual to which staff must refer. This corporate identity covers signs, headed paper, layout of letters – most forms of one-way communication.

Most of the brochures are produced corporately covering every one of the outlets in one big brochure, so as a consequence advertising is focused around the main brand rather than just part of it. Brochures and leaflets relating to local events and attractions will be dealt with by the in-house promotion managers at Centre level.

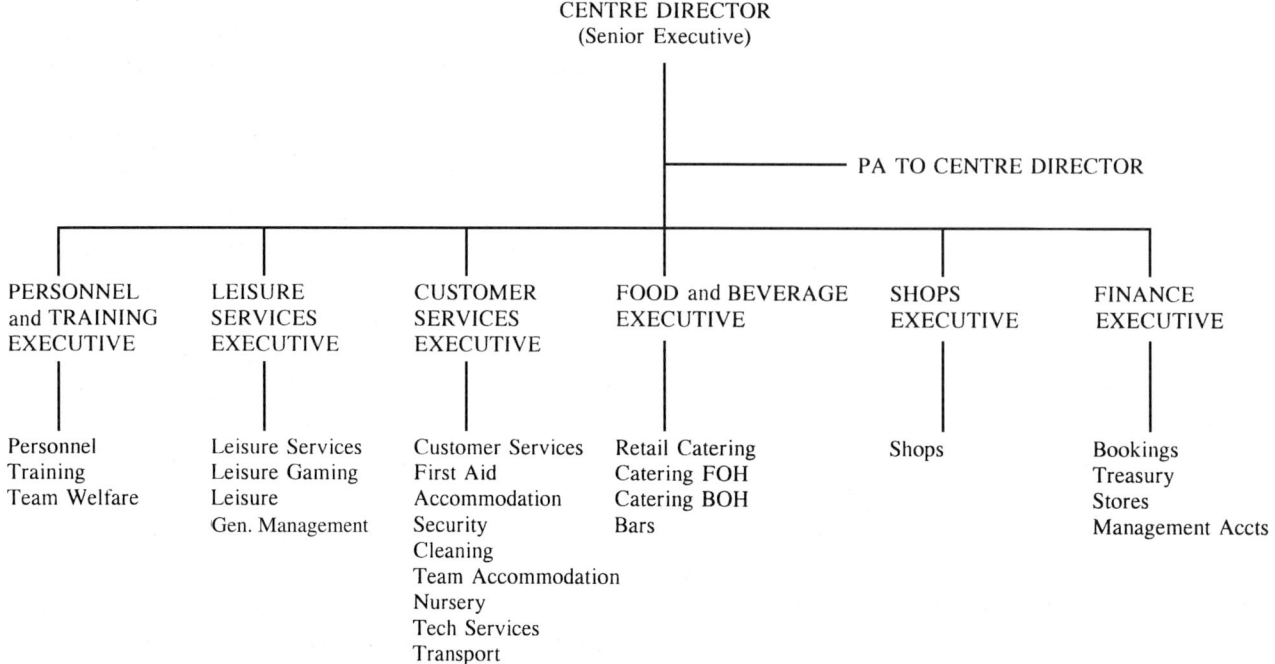

FIGURE 4.3 *Organisational Structure.*

A VISIT TO A HOLIDAY WORLD

In the Butlin's brochure is the statement:

> 'Where Customer Service is concerned, we are committed to making your holiday the best ever. That means our Team must be trained to a very high standard to be able to offer you the service you deserve! Our on-going Customer Care Training Programme – STARS – not only trains our new Team members but improves the service skills of our existing Team. The programme caters for all Team members, including Senior Management, and has already helped us win national awards and recognition from Training Enterprise Councils (TECs) and Tourist Authorities.'

Communication systems

There is a wide range of communication systems on the site, both one-way and two-way, internal and external:

- *one-way communication systems include* signs, notices, written correspondence and public-address systems. The layout of the signs and notices comply with the company image. The use of a sophisticated graphics software package means that all hand-written signs have been done away with, and some notices incorporate humorous graphics to underline the message
- *two-way systems include* face-to-face and telephone conversations, intercom systems, mobile radio – the latter systems being important for communication between staff across a large site to ensure a rapid response.

Electronic Technology
The introduction of electronic technology has enabled fast and efficient communication:

- the reservation system has been computerised (this system is discussed in more depth later)
- the computer system is networked to all buildings on the site
- all staff can be e-mailed internally. One manager commented on how he resisted e-mail initially, but when the e-mail went down once for a number of days, he was 'quite lost'. The speed of the e-mail is appreciated: it is faster than a letter or memo, and does not contribute to paper wastage. 'If someone should send a message – often just a few words can answer the query. It enables one message to be sent to selected groups; for example, the financial controller can send the same memo to all members of the executive at once'
- there is limited access to the Internet, although its use is growing. The IT Co-ordinator has been creating pages on the Internet to provide information on Butlin's for those who web-browse. As more people access the Internet, Southcoast World are considering direct job recruitment – it is felt this could be fast, accurate and save money.

As all machines are networked, all correspondence, graphical and statistical information, is saved on the mainframe. Nothing is saved on local machines. There is an approximate ratio of 2:1 users to machines. If someone has finished working on a computer, has saved their work, and then left the machine, the computer will allow someone else to use it after ten minutes on the entry 'menu' has passed, as long as they enter their personal identity code and password.

If for some reason there is a 'crash' such as through a computer fault, or a power supply failure, then the **file server** will keep the system alive for 20 minutes through the battery back-up. It will also send a signal to anyone on a machine that the power will be cut in a number of minutes.

A 'back-up' or second copy is made each night, and in the case of a 'crash' a back-up is made automatically.

The organisation is looking to the future

and reviewing new computer systems, both hardware and software, in order to update and ensure that all systems are compatible within the autonomous centre, and with the parent company. The aim is to have a system which is versatile and stable, with an integrated suite of word processors, spreadsheets, graphics, desktop publishing and a file server which are all talking the same language, and is year 2000 compatible. As the IT Co-ordinator pointed out, 'You need something which is going to stay up more than a day. When you lift up a car bonnet and change something, you may affect another part of the engine. Once it is running nicely and all the users are happy, and there are no quirks, then leave it alone. The only thing you need to do on a daily basis, and be absolutely regimented about, is your back-up.'

INFORMATION-PROCESSING SYSTEMS

The main information-processing systems are electronic, although there are some paper-based systems. For example, the shops, bars and restaurants currently inform the stores of their needs through a requisition spread sheet at the end of a day and the stock is delivered the next day. The organisation is moving towards direct computer links, so as stocks are used in the venues (see Figure 4.4), the information from the computerised tills will feed directly into the stock control section.

The stock system is drawn into an individual report which is part of the raw data provided on a regular basis for the manager's report and trading profits.

Electronic information-processing systems

As with any organisation, there is a constant updating of software and hardware.

In identifying the main impact of introducing information technology, the IT Co-ordinator commented on:

- the ability to store and retrieve information more easily – if this information is correct in the first place! There were instances of incorrect or incomplete information having been entered
- speed
- reliability
- how staff welcomed computers
- the ease of use of the new software such as Excel and Word Perfect
- although there had been no direct analysis of any saving in costs, staff realised that with the new technology they could do things better, and faster
- increase in productivity.

Reservation system

When you telephone to make a booking, your call goes to the central reservation system which deals with all the Butlin's Leisure Worlds. The receiver will lead you through a number of questions which mirror those on the booking form (see Figure 4.5). These questions deal with venue, type of accommodation needed, dates, number of people, whether travel insurance is needed, etc.

The receiver will check availability of accommodation, and if there is accommodation available then you will be asked if you wish to take the option of booking. You can pay immediately via credit or debit card, or book provisionally and pay within approximately five days, e.g. by cheque.

Every transaction from the previous day is followed up with 'reverse confirmation sheets'. Figure 4.6 is an example of a reverse confirmation sheet which gives full details so customers can check their bookings. You, as the customer, are then asked to post the form back as soon as possible as final confirmation of the holiday.

There are administrative functions on the booking form; there is a section allowing for special requests to be identified. There are also pre-typed receipt texts which detail any special requests – these appear on the reverse confirmation form.

A VISIT TO A HOLIDAY WORLD

FIGURE 4.4 *The stores have a requisition system to enable shops, bars and restaurants to order stocks for next day delivery so they can meet anticipated customer needs.*

FIGURE 4.5 *Booking Form.*

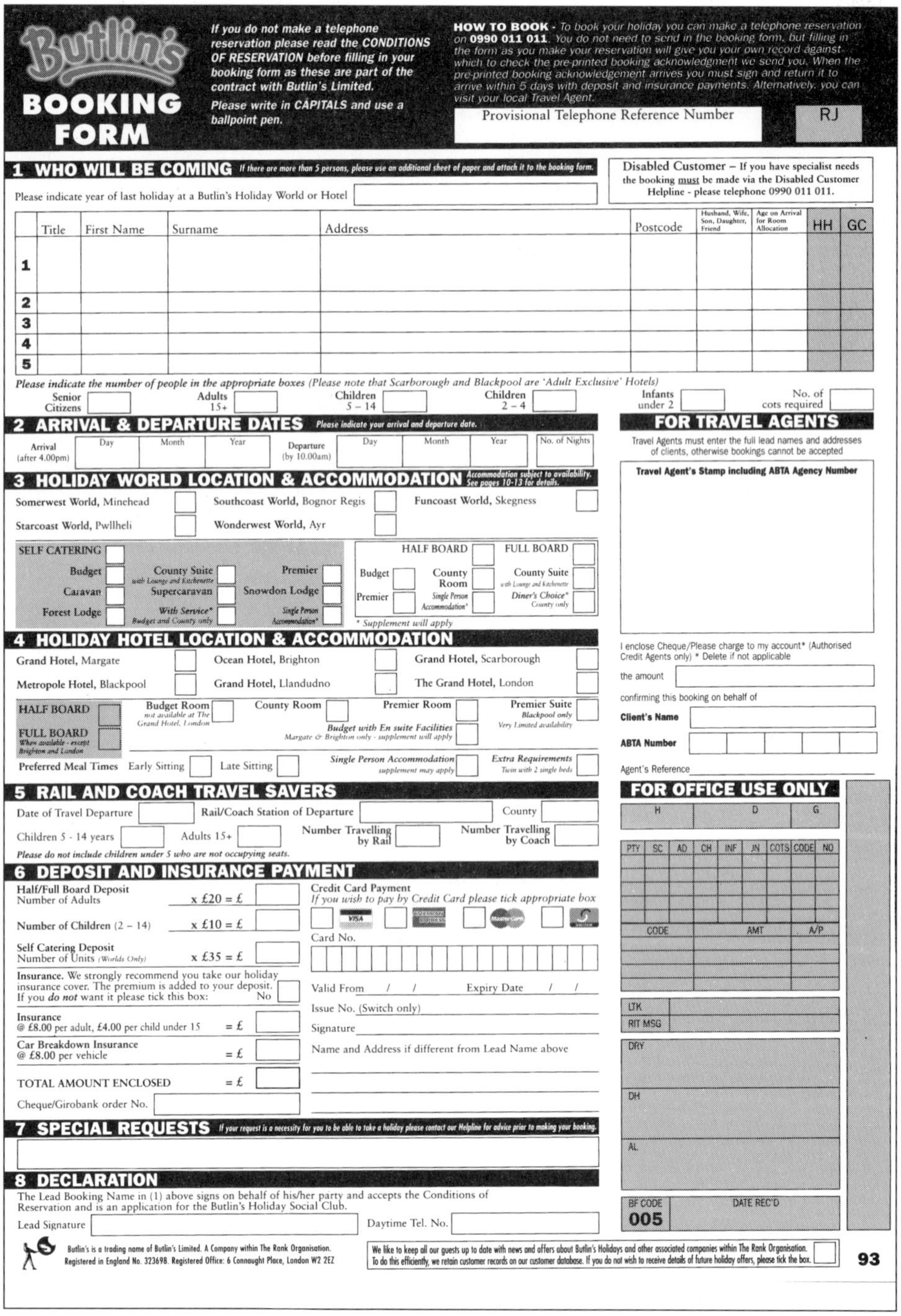

Butlin's BOOKING FORM

If you do not make a telephone reservation please read the CONDITIONS OF RESERVATION before filling in your booking form as these are part of the contract with Butlin's Limited.

Please write in CAPITALS and use a ballpoint pen.

HOW TO BOOK - *To book your holiday you can make a telephone reservation on* **0990 011 011**. *You do not need to send in the booking form, but filling in the form as you make your reservation will give you your own record against which to check the pre-printed booking acknowledgment we send you. When the pre-printed booking acknowledgement arrives you must sign and return it to arrive within 5 days with deposit and insurance payments. Alternatively, you can visit your local Travel Agent.*

Provisional Telephone Reference Number | RJ

1 WHO WILL BE COMING *If there are more than 5 persons, please use an additional sheet of paper and attach it to the booking form.*

Please indicate year of last holiday at a Butlin's Holiday World or Hotel

Disabled Customer – If you have specialist needs the booking must be made via the Disabled Customer Helpline - please telephone 0990 011 011.

	Title	First Name	Surname	Address	Postcode	Husband, Wife, Son, Daughter, Friend	Age on Arrival for Room Allocation	HH	GC
1									
2									
3									
4									
5									

Please indicate the number of people in the appropriate boxes (Please note that Scarborough and Blackpool are 'Adult Exclusive' Hotels)

Senior Citizens | Adults 15+ | Children 5 – 14 | Children 2 – 4 | Infants under 2 | No. of cots required

2 ARRIVAL & DEPARTURE DATES *Please indicate your arrival and departure date.*

Arrival (after 4.00pm) Day Month Year | Departure (by 10.00am) Day Month Year | No. of Nights

3 HOLIDAY WORLD LOCATION & ACCOMMODATION *Accommodation subject to availability. See pages 10-13 for details.*

Somerwest World, Minehead | Southcoast World, Bognor Regis | Funcoast World, Skegness

Starcoast World, Pwllheli | Wonderwest World, Ayr

SELF CATERING: Budget | County Suite *with Lounge and Kitchenette* | Premier | Caravan | Supercaravan | Snowdon Lodge | Forest Lodge | *With Service* Budget and County only* | *Single Person Accommodation**

HALF BOARD | FULL BOARD: Budget | County Room | County Suite *with Lounge and Kitchenette* | Premier | *Single Person Accommodation** | *Diner's Choice* County only*

** Supplement will apply*

4 HOLIDAY HOTEL LOCATION & ACCOMMODATION

Grand Hotel, Margate | Ocean Hotel, Brighton | Grand Hotel, Scarborough

Metropole Hotel, Blackpool | Grand Hotel, Llandudno | The Grand Hotel, London

HALF BOARD | FULL BOARD *When available - except Brighton and London*

Budget Room *not available at The Grand Hotel, London* | County Room | Premier Room | Premier Suite *Blackpool only Very Limited availability*

Budget with En suite Facilities *Margate & Brighton only - supplement will apply*

Preferred Meal Times Early Sitting | Late Sitting | *Single Person Accommodation supplement may apply* | *Extra Requirements Twin with 2 single beds*

5 RAIL AND COACH TRAVEL SAVERS

Date of Travel Departure | Rail/Coach Station of Departure | County

Children 5 - 14 years | Adults 15+ | Number Travelling by Rail | Number Travelling by Coach

Please do not include children under 5 who are not occupying seats.

6 DEPOSIT AND INSURANCE PAYMENT

Half/Full Board Deposit Number of Adults x £20 = £

Number of Children (2 – 14) x £10 = £

Self Catering Deposit Number of Units *(Worlds Only)* x £35 = £

Insurance. We strongly recommend you take our holiday insurance cover. The premium is added to your deposit. If you *do not* want it please tick this box: No

Insurance @ £8.00 per adult, £4.00 per child under 15 = £

Car Breakdown Insurance @ £8.00 per vehicle = £

TOTAL AMOUNT ENCLOSED = £

Cheque/Girobank order No.

Credit Card Payment *If you wish to pay by Credit Card please tick appropriate box*

VISA | AMERICAN EXPRESS | MasterCard | SWITCH

Card No.

Valid From / / Expiry Date / /

Issue No. (Switch only)

Signature

Name and Address if different from Lead Name above

7 SPECIAL REQUESTS *If your request is a necessity for you to be able to take a holiday please contact our Helpline for advice prior to making your booking.*

8 DECLARATION

The Lead Booking Name in (1) above signs on behalf of his/her party and accepts the Conditions of Reservation and is an application for the Butlin's Holiday Social Club.

Lead Signature | Daytime Tel. No.

FOR TRAVEL AGENTS

Travel Agents must enter the full lead names and addresses of clients, otherwise bookings cannot be accepted

Travel Agent's Stamp including ABTA Agency Number

I enclose Cheque/Please charge to my account* (Authorised Credit Agents only) * Delete if not applicable

the amount

confirming this booking on behalf of

Client's Name

ABTA Number

Agent's Reference

FOR OFFICE USE ONLY

H | D | G

PTY | SC | AD | CH | INF | JN | COTS | CODE | NO

CODE | AMT | A/P

LTK

RIT MSG

DRY

DH

AL

BF CODE 005 | DATE REC'D

Butlin's is a trading name of Butlin's Limited. A Company within The Rank Organisation. Registered in England No. 323698. Registered Office: 6 Connaught Place, London W2 2EZ

We like to keep all our guests up to date with news and offers about Butlin's Holidays and other associated companies within The Rank Organisation. To do this efficiently, we retain customer records on our customer database. If you do not wish to receive details of future holiday offers, please tick the box.

93

The booking office keeps data for internal use, for instance a customer's age, gender and type of any discount claimed may be recorded. This data will go through to the marketing section for analysis. One problem that hinders analysis is that some customers do not fully complete their booking forms or their 'reverse confirmations'.

There have so far been three reservations systems in use. A member of staff in the bookings office commented that the current one is much more user friendly, and meets the needs of customers and staff. It is also efficient, fast and reliable. 'The customers should not notice that much of a difference – it is more efficient for us so the customer should receive that benefit.'

There is encouragement for payment to be

A VISIT TO A HOLIDAY WORLD

FIGURE 4.6 *Reverse Confirmation Sheet.*

Butlin's Ltd.
P.O. Box 96
Bognor Regis
PO21 1YE
Telephone: (0990) 033033

BOOKING REFERENCE
YA / 94 / 2 / 6-267 571-8P

Please read the conditions of reservation and the important notes as these form part of the contract with Butlin's Ltd.

Butlin's HOLIDAYS

THIS IS NOT A V.A.T. INVOICE

DEAR MR   Date: 5 March 1997

Thank you for booking your Butlin's holiday. This letter confirms your booking arrangements. Please sign below to confirm the details are correct. If not, let us know and we will send you a corrected confirmation. Complete the lower section of the reverse side and return with any outstanding amounts by 15 MAR 1997.

HOLIDAY DATES
ARRIVE (for check-in after 16:00 hours): SATURDAY – 12 APR 1997
ACCOMMODATION VACATED (by 10:00 hours): MONDAY – 14 APR 1997

PARTY SIZE
Senior Citizen: 0   Adult: 30   Child: 43
Junior: 0   Infant: 2   Cots: 2

ACCOMMODATION
a Self Catering County Suite
12 × 1 Double & 2 Singles – 2 Bedrooms
5 × 1 Double & 3 Singles – 3 Bedrooms

HOLIDAY COST   AMOUNT
Basic Price Includes VAT   1843.00

SUPPLEMENTS

DISCOUNTS
Large Party   −276.45
Large Party Free Place   −44.20

TRAVEL DETAILS
The number of travelling customers does not include the accompanied children in your party under five years old who travel free.

TOTAL HOLIDAY COST   1522.35
TOTAL AMOUNT PAID   0.00
AMOUNT DUE BY 15 MAR 1997   1522.35

The above amount due can be paid by returning the completed lower section of this letter with your payment details.

NO TRAVEL HAS BEEN ARRANGED WITH BUTLINS

IMPORTANT NOTES:

The price of your holiday includes the VAT charge at the prevailing rate. We reserve the right to reflect any increase in VAT rate in holiday prices.

This booking is not confirmed until we have received the completed confirmation tear off below. Please post this to us by return to ensure your booking is confirmed.

WE HOPE YOU HAVE A WONDERFUL STAY WITH US
YOURS SINCERELY   BOOKINGS MANAGER.

✂ - ✂
REMITTANCE ADVANCE: Please return this part with the payment due.

Ref: YA / 94 / 2 / 6-267 571-8P
AMOUNT DUE BY 15 MAR 1997   1522.35

Payment method   Mastercard ☐   Visa ☐   American Express ☐   Switch ☐
(please tick)   Card No: ☐☐☐☐ ☐☐☐☐ ☐☐☐☐ ☐☐☐☐
                  Valid From: ☐☐-☐☐ to ☐☐-☐☐ Issue: ☐☐
                  Credit card holder's name, address & signature if different from lead name:
                  _____
                  _____
                  _____
ABTA: _____
REF: _____

BATCH: Or Cheque/Giro Bank/Postal Order NO: _____
BFC: 986   Amount Enclosed £_____
                  If you do not wish to receive details of future offers from both
                  ourselves and other associated companies within the Rank Group Plc.
                  plese tick the box and return this letter to the address shown ☐
I HAVE READ AND ACCEPTED THE CONDITIONS   BUTLIN'S LIMITED: REGISTERED IN ENGLAND UNDER NO. 323698 A COMPANY WITHIN THE RANK GROUP PLC
OF RESERVATIONS ON REVERSE SIDE.
SIGNATURE: _____

Ref: YA /94/ 2 / 6-267 571-8P

---

made by credit and debit cards. This means that bookings and financial transactions can be reconciled more quickly. However, the company still deals with a great many cheques.

The booking forms are used more by the travel trade. Direct customers tend to telephone in, and many do not necessarily see the brochure.

On arrival

Virtually all customers will have paid before they arrive and this minimises the handling of transactions on arrival. There are two areas/desks that take cash:

- *unpaid balances* – for anyone who has made late amendments and has not paid the difference

BUSINESS SYSTEMS FOR LEISURE AND TOURISM

FIGURE 4.7 *Customer Service is seen as a priority at Southcoast World where there is a Customer Service point. Customer Service staff have good communication links with all sections of Southcoast World so they can deal with any enquiries efficiently.*

- *customer service* – which deals with customers who arrive at the centre and want to change the nature of their accommodation (see Figure 4.7). Availability is checked, and if changes can be accommodated then payment is taken.

There are facilities to take all types of payment: cash, cheques, postal orders, credit and debit card.

When customers arrive they go to the reception area. Staff are there to welcome visitors, provide information and give out welcome packages.

To ensure that customer waiting time is kept to a minimum they are directed to specific desk numbers. At certain times of the year, particularly Christmas, customers tend to arrive at approximately the same time, so there could be 10,000 people going through at a peak period and this can prove a challenge to all staff, and all administrative systems.

There are information booths around the site with staff who can deal with general questions.

Day visitors

Day visitors pay at the entry point. The ticketing system, which is a touch screen not a keyboard, can create one ticket for groups either immediately at the gate – which can save the time of printing a large number of individual tickets – or the tickets can be pre-ordered. The system speeds the service for customers and helps reduce queues.

EXTERNAL QUALITY STANDARDS

Southcoast World was the first company in Sussex, and the first leisure company in the UK, to gain an Investors in People Award (IIP) in 1991. The IIP award mirrored the growing belief in the company of the need to invest in training for staff at all levels:

'Our prime objective is the ultimate customer experience, and everything we are doing in developing and underpinning our people is aimed at that one prime objective.

And of course, after that objective, greater profitability ... we must not be afraid to say it – we need to make a profit in this game' (Personnel Director).

The organisation considered the Quality Standard BS EN ISO 9000, but felt IIP was more appropriate as it was a people-based quality measure. They felt that BS EN ISO 9000 would probably be more appropriate if they were involved in production and everything was more easily measurable and quantifiable, but felt it less appropriate for a service-based industry.

A member of the Personnel and Training Department commented that it 'was not just down to IIP but down to the whole cultural shift and cultural change as Southcoast World became a training focused organisation, with a managerial commitment, which is based upon allowing individuals time for training and development'.

At Southcoast World the organisation established its own Training and Development Centre (see Figure 4.8), providing training for staff in a wide range of occupational areas: administration, customer service, food hygiene, personnel, management, IT, banking. Many of these are linked to national awards such as **National Vocational Qualifications (NVQs)**.

Through their monitoring procedures, the organisation has experienced:

- a year-on-year reduction of complaints from customers. This follows a monitoring of customer satisfaction through questionnaires
- a reduction of two-thirds in the turn-over of staff in the last six years, since 1990
- a rise to the top of the ranking system (based on profitability) across the whole of the organisation.

The organisation strongly believes that in the service-based industries, such as leisure and tourism, the only way to develop the product is to develop the people. 'At the end of the day the face-to-face contact between the individual and the customer will make or break the product'.

FIGURE 4.8 *In-house training for staff at Southcoast World.*

SECTION 5

A Visit to a Theme Park

CASE STUDY: *LEGOLAND®*

Key Aims

> In this section you will be examining a case study of a leisure park based on a specific theme. You will consider:
>
> - the structure of the organisation
> - the business systems they operate in order to meet the needs of their customers, particularly the booking and admissions systems.

INTRODUCTION

Legoland is a family theme park located in 150 acres of wooded landscape near Windsor.

The Legoland group, owned and managed by the Kirk Christiansen family of Billund, Denmark, comprises 50 companies in 29 countries on six continents. It has a total of 9,200 employees, 50 per cent of whom are in Denmark. The business is run under the motto 'Only the best is good enough'.

The first one outside Denmark (see Figure 5.1), at Windsor, was opened in the spring of 1996. The third Legoland Park is scheduled to open in 1999 in the United States.

A VISIT TO A THEME PARK

FIGURE 5.1 *Miniland is the heart of Legoland Windsor and is made from over 20 million standard bricks. Pictured here is Brighton Pier.*

From the 'idea' through to completion of the Park at Windsor, the process involved a series of steps stringently followed in order to achieve the overall mission of Legoland Development:

> *To be the preferred choice of children and their families as a result of delivering exceptional value and the highest standards of quality, care, service and safety in the leisure industry.*
>
> *Legoland Windsor will be the ultimate LEGO clubhouse, not only for LEGO fans. It will be a world of enjoyable learning, family interaction and fun, and the most exuberant play environment.*

All operations and systems – including business systems – have been introduced in order that the organisation can meet this aim.

There are five activity theme areas in the Park in 40 acres of the site. There are more than 40 interactive rides, shows and attractions (see Figures 5.3 and 5.4 on pages 40 and 41). The park is open from March to September, and employs 75 full-time staff and 600 seasonal staff, primarily from the local area.

There are five restaurants/cafés in the Park, and a further 11 catering stalls. There are retail shops selling items such as toys, souvenirs, clothing and books.

There were 1.4 million visitors in the first year, the estimated time for a visit being more than 6 hours.

The business systems which have been set in place are to achieve the stated mission for the organisation, to enable it meet the needs of its customers, and be profitable.

Administrative systems are as paperless as possible; there is an emphasis on electronic technology and information-processing systems.

ELECTRONIC TECHNOLOGY

There are two office systems with different file servers:

- *administration*, using a Windows generating system
- *bookings* – this system is very specialised and can produce management reports from the data held.

The Accounts Section can take data from both systems.

All permanent personnel have their own computers. Software packages include word processing, spreadsheets, databases. Different sections have their own specific software. Group Sales have a sales tracking system, Personnel have a system for payroll.

Most computers are networked into one of the systems, with restricted access so only appropriate people can access specific information.

All computers are backed-up every night. If there is an interruption in the power supply, then there is a ten-minute period when all information can be saved.

As all technology has been purchased in the last year, they do not envisage difficulties arising in the year 2000 when problems may occur with some information-processing systems.

BOOKING SYSTEM

Guests can purchase tickets in advance by telephone, paying by credit or debit card, and the booking system is linked to a credit card clearance system. There is therefore no need for these customers to queue when they arrive at the Park; they will be guaranteed entry even on the busiest day.

This service acts as a planning tool as the organisation knows in advance approximate numbers which can be expected in any one day, and this information can be extrapolated into estimates for **walk-up business**. The forecast enables the organisation to plan staffing, and restaurants can order sufficient fresh food to meet anticipated demands.

The sophisticated software system was designed specifically for the theme park. There is a call centre with operators answering queries and taking bookings. When all the lines are busy, the call is automatically diverted to an overflow system at an agency. The data is then transferred from the agency back to Legoland, who will either send out the tickets by post to customers or hold them at the entrance gate for their arrival.

Following an evaluation of the system, to assist in collecting data and shorten call time, Legoland implemented a 'quick address system': the caller is asked for their post code and the receiver then checks the correct address against details held on a database. Details are entered into the correct field in the database so that it appears in correct post office approved format, 'so the address on the envelope becomes 99 per cent accurate'. This processing of information helps in terms of speed, so there is an increase in the number of telephone calls and transactions which can be dealt with.

Organisations can now purchase a 'quick address' system which not only matches the post code against address, but against the name on the electoral roll. The caller need only give his or her post code and number of the road and the organisation has the correct spelling of their name. Legoland felt that this system was not appropriate as:

- electoral rolls go out of date as people move
- customers may not be comfortable with the idea of so much data being held and used.

As the system was being developed, and in the first year of use, there was evaluation of the system as it was important it worked efficiently so that customer needs could be met. The system is monitored regularly and adjusted to ensure optimum efficiency.

There is an in-house information technology team, and there are external maintenance contracts.

A VISIT TO A THEME PARK

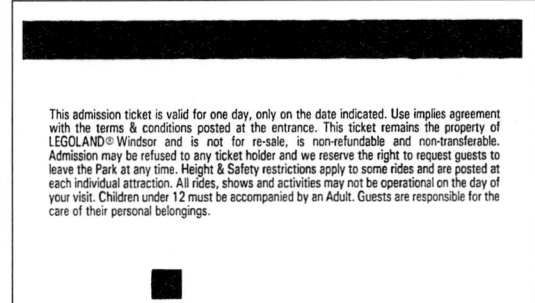

FIGURE 5.2 *Each ticket has a picture of a Legoland character on the front and conditions of entry on the back.*

Training was provided for staff using the booking system, and this varied according to the different needs and experience of staff.

ADMISSION SYSTEM

Any ticket purchased will be encoded for a specific day (see Figure 5.2). When a customer puts this ticket through the main park turnstile the number will be matched against either the purchase that day or against the advanced booking entry. This system is linked to an accounts system which tracks payment of tickets.

A proportion of the business is group bookings and there are facilities to deal with these through an invoicing procedure. There are credit facilities for group bookings.

RETAIL

The information-processing system the Park uses feeds retail information to the accounting part of the admission system. The accounts team have information on retail sales which then helps VAT calculations, and provision of adequate supplies.

The system keeps track of payments for products through the tills in the four retail shops, and also links to a warehouse system for stock control. It allows the warehouse team to know how much is to be delivered each morning. Catering is on the same system so that the right quantity of fresh food can be ordered and delivered. A Swiss company, Movenpick Marche, are the on-site catering consultants . All food is fresh, with only the ice-cream being frozen. Local suppliers are used whenever possible.

PAPER-BASED SYSTEMS

The paper-based systems that do operate are often linked to electronic information-processing systems. The three following examples illustrate this.

- At the end of a day all staff responsible for ticket sales cash up and generate a report on sales for that day. There is a printout from the ticket machine. Staff then complete a paper summary, checking that the cash in the till matches the printout from the machine. Both reports are then taken to the cash office which checks both the printout and the summary sheet
- One of the responsibilities for a member of staff on duty at each of the rides will be to note, with a 'click' on a small machine, each customer who uses the ride. Each hour s/he will record the number for that hour on a paper chart. At the end of the day this information is logged into a computer from the paper chart. This enables the organisation to analyse the flow of customers using rides
- Correspondence (guest letters) is responded to rapidly, frequently by letter, and a hard copy will be filed. However, details are logged into a computerised system so that there can be tracking of types of letters received and of the responses made

COMMUNICATION

Good communication is seen as the key to an effective and efficient organisation which meets customer needs. There are weekly operations meetings with representatives from each departmental team:

- Marketing and Sales
- Operations, which includes attractions, retail, security, entertainment
- Admissions
- Catering
- Personnel

FIGURE 5.3 *Children can learn driving skills, and earn their very own Legoland Driving Licence.*

A VISIT TO A THEME PARK

- Information Technology
- Logistics
- Inventory Management, which includes stock control
- Technical Services

The Park at Windsor has CC mail, which is an internal version of e-mail. Those using the e-mail system have found it valuable.

Three computers on site have access to the Internet, and the LEGO Group has its own Internet site. The group is looking at the World Wide Intranet, a world wide communication system specific to the LEGO group. Legoland at Windsor could then communicate more directly with sales offices for LEGO toys in over 20 countries for marketing purposes. Currently they use the fax, telephone or postal system.

The voice mail system is actively used. If a member of staff is unable to take a call, or is already using the telephone, then a recorded message can be left. Every 15–20 minutes the potential receiver of the message will be reminded that there are messages waiting to be listened to.

The staff handbook contains details of the standard format to be used for letters, memos, notices, signs, etc. This means that all one-way systems of communication meet the standards laid down, and are in keeping with the company image.

Some groups on the site can only be reached by internal memo. Copies are saved in the computer system, with a hard copy filed.

Although video-conferencing is not currently available at Legoland Windsor, they did have this facility while the Park was being built. Meetings could then be held with the parent company in Denmark in this developmental phase.

There is a telephone at each ride, shop and restaurant. To aid communication between staff moving around the theme park mobile radios are used. Priority users are security guards and supervisory staff. There are four separate radio channels. If a member of staff

FIGURE 5.4 *Fairytale figures oversee modern entertainment: Prince Charming by the Fairy Tale Brook ride.*

has problems getting through to a specific person, then they contact a base number for assistance.

STAFF TRAINING

There is a training programme for all staff, both permanent and seasonal, and there are dedicated training rooms on site. All training is in-house and there is a heavy emphasis on customer service, and health and safety – reflecting the emphasis in the main aims of the Park. New staff will be introduced to the way of working – the LEGO way – during their induction programme. Not only will they need to know the appropriate business systems which operate, they also need to understand the culture of the organisation.

The staff handbook, which gives staff details of administrative and communication systems, also explains the organisation's expectations of staff, such as appropriate appearance.

MAINTAINING QUALITY STANDARDS

The organisation has not introduced any voluntary external quality standard, but has set its own internal standards. The emphasis of the mission is to deliver 'exceptional value and the highest standards of quality, care, service and safety in the leisure industry'; there are therefore procedures in place to monitor the systems and facilities. When monitoring the quality of administrative, communication or information-processing systems, not only are problems dealt with as they arise, but staff are encouraged to suggest improvements.

Health and safety

Health and safety, as emphasised in the aim of the organisation, is carefully monitored. Extensive safety checks are run every morning.

Although there is no legal capacity limit, the organisation decided that they would set a limited capacity in the park to keep numbers comfortable for children as most of their visitors are families with younger children. The information gained from the advanced booking service therefore affects the number admitted to the Park from walk-up business, and staff on the gate are given a cut-off point figure daily.

Environment

Although not registered for BS 7750 Environmental Management, the organisation is aware of its impact on the local environment. Changes have been made to roads and traffic flow to minimise disturbance. Only the central 45 acres has been developed, leaving parkland as a buffer zone. There is close working with the local environmental health officer and other relevant local authority bodies such as the Royal Windsor Information Centre.

SECTION 6

Consultancy

CASE STUDY

KIRKHAM HOTEL

Key Aims

> In this section you will act as a consultant to a developing hotel which needs advice. You will:
> - draw upon the skills and knowledge you already have relating to business systems
> - evaluate the business systems
> - make recommendations.

Eight years ago Peter and Eileen Burns decided that they would let out a number of rooms on a commercial basis as bed and breakfast accommodation. They had a large house with five bedrooms and felt that they could easily let out three. They made changes, such as ensuring that they met health and safety requirements. They called the business Kirkham Guest House.

Peter and Eileen shared the responsibilities. For example, Peter undertook to cook breakfast, and Eileen to deal with laundry. Both dealt with bookings. When anyone telephoned to reserve a room the details were written into a reservations book. If Peter or Eileen were busy, their son or daughter took the telephone call and left a message for their parents. The business was a family affair. They put small advertisements in the local paper and were on the local Tourist Office

FIGURE 6.1 *Kirkham Hotel.*

register. All letters to customers or suppliers were hand-written. Payment was requested by cash or cheque – credit cards were not accepted.

Over the last four years the two adjoining properties came up for sale and Peter and Eileen purchased these. They invested money in uniting the three properties and upgrading rooms, and they now have 20 rooms for commercial use.

They also felt that they could make better use of their catering and dining room facilities by offering lunches and evening meals – particularly for residents.

Staffing

At the beginning of their business venture the work was done by John, Eileen and their two teenage children. They employed a friend on an hourly basis to assist with cleaning and cooking.

When they purchased the first adjoining property they employed an additional person on an hourly basis, mainly to help in the kitchen in the mornings.

With 20 rooms, and restaurant facilities, Peter and Eileen realised that they could not continue with their previous staffing level, particularly as their children had left home. They now employ:

- three part-time staff: two cleaners and one waitress
- one full-time receptionist/administrative assistant (Sam)
- one full-time chef (Les).

Peter helps the chef in the kitchen, and Eileen is involved in both front of house and in administration. Only the chef has formal qualifications which were gained 15 years ago.

They are aware that there will need to be some changes, and one of these may be the investment in a computer – although Peter and Eileen dislike technology. This need to review how they operate has been underlined by comments in letters from customers and suppliers, and in their visitors' book. These can be seen in Figure 6.2.

Reservations

When a letter is received, Eileen or Sam check the reservation book and then write back to the prospective guest to confirm the booking. They also enclose a map. If there is a telephone booking, this is verbally confirmed immediately. A written confirmation and map is then sent to the prospective guest. Sam has some keyboard skills and Eileen is considering whether to purchase a typewriter, or a computer with a word processing package.

Care is taken to ensure confidentiality. The reservation book is not kept in full view of guests walking through the hotel.

Dealing with guests on their arrival

Usually Eileen or Sam is available to meet guests. Occasionally Peter will cover if needed. He can easily read Eileen's writing, but has occasional problems reading Sam's.

In the entrance hall is a display of information leaflets about local attractions. These are set out so that guests can easily find the leaflets they want.

> *Letter from guest*
> ... the atmosphere was excellent, and I enjoyed the company of other guests. However, I feel that the food was not up to the standard described in your glossy leaflet, and the waitress was uncertain of how to serve correctly.
>
> *Letter from guest*
> I arrived at the Kirkham Hotel on Friday night to find that there had been a mix-up of rooms. I had been assured of a room with a double bed, but when I arrived you only had a twin-bedded room left. The receptionist, who I believe was new, was not very helpful and spent a great deal of time going through the book to find the details.
>
> *Letter from Peter and Eileen's accountant*
> Thank you for the papers you sent me. I would have liked them sooner as I find it takes quite a lot of time to sort out the figures for the tax office, and we are getting close to the deadline date.
> Do you want me to draw up the graphs showing trading details as I did last year: profit compared with previous years, usage of the restaurant, number of guests per week? I am afraid I now need to charge an additional £500 for this service. I will telephone you to discuss this.
>
> *Note through door from local retailer*
> I tried to telephone you yesterday, Thursday, to let you know it will not be possible to get the fresh salmon you need for Saturday – your telephone line is constantly busy! Will trout be suitable as a substitute? Give me a call.
> NB: Have you ever thought about investing in a fax – we could probably contact each other more easily!
>
> *Comments in the visitors' book:*
>
> - Good selection of wine. Rooms very clean. I wish the hotel accepted credit cards
> - I appreciated all the information you had about local attractions. The leaflets were nicely displayed, and I found them very helpful
> - Good English breakfast, but I do like butter on my toast – not margarine (no butter available on Thursday morning!)
> - Thank you. I enjoyed my stay. I am glad you sent me details of the special weekend offer
>
> *Note of telephone call from wholesaler*
> I received your message about needing oil, butter and coffee urgently. I can let you have the oil and coffee in the quantities you want, but only 20 kg of butter instead of the 40 kg you ordered. I will get the rest to you next week.

FIGURE 6.2 *Extracts from letters and the visitors' book.*

When guests leave

Guests pay by cheque or by cash, and a receipt is written out for them. Not all guests want a receipt, and occasionally Eileen or Sam do not write one. Details are later recorded in a ledger by Eileen.

Restaurant

There has been a steady growth in the number of guests staying at the hotel, and occasionally staff have difficulty in dealing with all the people. Peter and his chef try to vary the menus as much as possible. However, at times they are constrained by the supplies they have available in the kitchen. One morning guests were not able to have the usual option of smoked kippers as there were none left in kitchen. No one has responsibility for checking on stock. If stocks appear to be getting low, then Peter or Les will make a note of this for whoever is ringing the suppliers.

Communication

Letters are still hand-written, and some guests have appreciated what they have seen as a 'personal touch'.

Peter and Eileen have records of addresses of all previous guests. Occasionally they send out hotel details, and information on special offer weekends. Addresses are kept in an alphabetical card system which is easy to access. Envelopes are hand-written by Peter, Eileen or Sam.

Within the hotel there are clear signs giving directions to guest rooms, to the restaurant and the lounge.

Staff pay

Payment to their full-time staff is monthly and made directly from the hotel bank account. Payment to part-time staff is by cash at the end of each week.

Payment of invoices

The majority of invoices are paid by cheque at the end of each month. Occasionally a local supplier will be paid in cash if there is sufficient in the till. Details are entered in the accounts book by Eileen.

Analysis of information

In the past Peter and Eileen have asked their accountant to analyse information and present this in a visual form. Neither Peter nor Eileen feel that they have the skills, nor the time, to draw up this analysis, even in a simple form. As the accountant's fees are rising they are considering what to do next.

Eileen regularly reviews income and expenditure and last year did draw up, by hand, a simple graph to show the 'highs' and 'lows' relating to income.

Peter has a form which he fills in to record the number of people using the restaurant at lunch time and in the evening. He feels the system is easy to use, even when he is busy.

Although Peter and Eileen are aware that they need to review, and update, their business systems they do not want to be pushed into introducing too much technology which could change the nature of the relationship with their guests. They accept that a computer could possibly help in a number of areas, but some systems are working well and need not be altered. They are also concerned about the high cost of introducing technology and whether this can be justified.

CONSULTANCY

TASK 14

You have been asked to evaluate the business systems at the Kirkham Hotel by the owners. They have asked for a written report which looks at all their business systems. They would also like you to make recommendations.

A member of your team has visited the hotel and obtained the background and details of its current operations – you have read this report on pages 43–46.

1 Write a report for the owners which will include:
   - an evaluation of the business systems
   - recommendations

2 When looking at the business systems, remember to comment on the:
   - administrative system
   - communication system
   - information-processing system

3 In your evaluation you need to consider:
   - fitness for purpose
   - value for money
   - accuracy
   - efficiency
   - security
   - ease of use
   - user opinion

4 When suggesting any possible improvements to any of the systems, include consideration of:
   - procedures
   - level of staff skills/expertise
   - equipment

When you are considering communication systems make recommendations relating to access to communications if it is appopriate.

You will be drawing upon the notes you made during Sections 1, 2 and 3.

Key Skills Hint: Writing a Report

When writing a formal report with recommendations, remember to prepare before you start writing. Consider:

- What is the purpose of the report?
- What type of report should it be?
- What is the readership? Is the person who requested the report the only reader? Who else will see the report? What can readers be expected to know about the subject

Gather and collate the information

Some form of research or data collection may be needed, and you may need to read other reports, interview people, gather data from different locations. In this way you will gain a balanced picture of the subject.

Structure the report

Plan the layout. The following simple framework can form the basis of most reports:

- Introduction (to include terms of reference)
- Summary
- Main report
- Conclusion
- Recommendations
- Supplementary evidence (including full tables and figures)

Writing the report

- Keep the message simple
- Write positively
- Avoid long and complicated sentences
- Include only information the reader needs to know
- Only use technical terms when unavoidable. You may need to include a glossary if the readers are not experts in the subject

Graphs and visuals are helpful for explaining complex information.

Review what you have written.

Useful Addresses

British Standards Institute (BSI)
389 Chiswick High Road
London W4 4AL

Investors in People Scotland
13 Abercromby Place
Edinburgh EH3 6LB

The National Accreditation Council for Certification Bodies (NACCB)
Audley House
13 Palace Street
London SW1E 5HS

The Environment Council
21 Elizabeth Street
London SW1W 9RP

Institute of Ecology and Environmental Management
36 Kingfisher Court
Hambridge Road
Newbury
Berkshire RG14 5UP

Health and Safety Executive Information Centre
Broad Lane
Sheffield S3 7HQ

NCVQ
222 Euston Road
London NW1 2BZ

Glossary

Administrative systems: systems which are in place to support routine and non-routine functions relating to financial, human and physical resources.

Baseline: a starting point.

British Standards Institute (BSI): a national organisation for ensuring quality of products.

BS 7750 Environment management: a quality standard which focuses on the impact of an organisation on the environment.

BS EN ISO 9000: a quality standard which focuses on the consistency of the end product or service.

Business systems: systems set in place to ensure that customer needs are met, and include administrative, communication and information-processing systems.

Communication systems: the provision of internal and external channels for exchanging information.

Computer network: a number of individual computers connected to a central point for shared use of programmes and information.

Computer reservation system: a database which contains information about availability, prices, customer details, etc.

Customer service information: when an organisation responds to external enquirers.

Data Protection Act 1984: this Act gave the individual the right to access information held in computer databases containing personal information, and the right to have such information held securely.

Database: computer software which enables the storage and retrieval of information such as names and addresses of customers, members, suppliers.

Desktop publishing: a computer software package which enables the publishing of documents, such as leaflets, which can be laid out in different way, with different fonts, incorporating images, etc.

Electronic information-processing system: an information-processing system usually controlled by a computer.

E-mail (electronic mail): a computer based system which allows the transmission of information directly from one registered e-mail user to another.

Enhanced telephone system: the telephone system has extensions such as fax, modems, Internet.

European Commission: a group of people, appointed by agreement by the governments of the European Community, who initiate action and look after its treaties.

External communication channels: ways of ensuring that there is an exchange of information with organisations and individuals outside an organisation.

Fax: an enhanced telephone system which allows the transmission of documents via a telephone line.

File server: a software package which controls the flow of information and access to other software packages and to files on a networked computer system. It aids security and also ensures access by appropriate personnel through passwords.

Fitness for purpose: whether a system does what it is supposed to do.

Full-board accommodation: bed and all meals provided.

Graphics: computer software programme which can be used to produce illustrations, drawings, diagrams.

Half-board accommodation: bed, breakfast and evening meal.

Hardware: the physical equipment, such as the printer, VDU, keyboard, mouse, scanner.

Information-processing system: a manual or

GLOSSARY

electronic based system of processing information about the organisation and its customers. The system can receive and store information and allow appropriate people to retrieve this when needed.

Internal communication channels: ways of ensuring that there is an exchange of information within and across an organisation.

International Standards Organisation (ISO): an external quality standard which is usually issued by different countries or groups of countries.

Internet: an enhanced telephone system which enables users to access information on databases.

Investors in People (IIP): a national quality standard which focuses on the training and development of all staff.

Keyboard: computer hardware which is used to input data into a computer.

Management Information System (MIS): a system which enables the collection, collation, storage, retrieval, analysis, and use of data to support the management and planning of an organisation.

Manual information-processing system: an information-processing system in which the information may be written by hand and includes paper-based systems such as cash books, hand-written booking forms.

Modem: an enhanced telephone system which enables computers to speak to each other using a telephone link.

Mouse: Manually Operated User Signal Encoder which is used to input data into a computer.

National Vocational Qualification (NVQ): a national award designed for the training and assessment of people at work.

Non-routine functions: these are the more unusual, irregular functions such as dealing with accidents or emergencies, producing occasional information.

One-way communication: when information is given in one direction only, and there is no immediate response to the message given.

Quality assurance: process of ensuring that a product, service or facility meets customer requirements.

Quality control: the monitoring of the quality of the end product or service.

Quality standards: standards which detail the level of quality to be met.

Reservation system: a system which enables an organisation to process a request from a customer such as for tickets or accommodation. These are then 'reserved' on behalf of the customer.

Routine functions: day-to-day functions such as dealing with customer enquiries, dealing with and recording cash transactions.

Scanner: computer hardware which can copy text, graphics or photographs into a computer's memory.

Self-catering accommodation: sleeping accommodation is provided, but no meals.

Software: computer programmes, or applications, which enable the users to perform functions such as word processing.

Spreadsheet: computer software which enables the user to process and present numbers.

Statutory: required by law.

Touch screen: the use of a computer screen by touch rather than using a keyboard or mouse.

Training and Enterprise Councils (TECs): regional organisations set up by government to promote training and enterprise in the local area.

Two-way communication: there is both sending and receiving of a message, with interaction between sender and receiver.

Value Added Tax (VAT): the tax a company adds to specific products when they sell them to customers. The company then passes the amount of this tax to the government.

Value for money: whether a system is cost effective.

Video conferencing: the method by which a group of people in different geographical places are able to speak to, and see each other, on screens.

Visual Display Unit (VDU): computer hardware which displays the data on a screen.

Voice comprehension and generation: electronic technology which can understand simple oral messages, and create simple answers.

Walk-up business: day visitors to a leisure or theme park who have not booked in advance.

Word processing: computer software which can produce letters, reports, tables of figures.

Index

administrative systems   ix, 4–8, 50
   Legoland   37
admission system, Legoland   39

back-office activities   18, 19
Blue Flag criteria   2
booking systems   19–20
   Butlin's Southcoast World   30–3
   Legoland   38–9
British Standards Institute (BSI)   2, 50
BS 7750 Environmental Management   3–4, 5, 50
BS EN ISO 9000   2, 3, 5, 50
business systems   ix, 50
Butlin's Southcoast World   ix, x, 7, 11, 13, 17, 26–35
   accommodation choices   27–8
   arrivals   33–4
   communication systems   29–30
   day visitors   34
   external quality standards   34–5
   information-processing systems   30–4
   organisational structure   30
   staff training   42

card indexes   20, 23
cash books   20
charts   20
communication systems   ix–x, 9–15, 50
   Butlin's Southcoast World   29–30
   electronic technology and   12–14
   Kirkham Hotel   46
   Legoland   40–2
corporate identity manual   28

customer service information   17, 50

Data Protection Act (1984)   23–4, 50
databases   viii, 21–2, 50
desktop publishing   22, 50

electronic information-processing systems   20–5, 50
   Butlin's Southcoast World   30–4
electronic mail (e-mail)   12–13, 29, 41, 50
electronic technology   12–14
   Butlin's Southcoast World   29–30
   and information-processing systems   16
   Legoland   38–9
European Commission (EC)   2

file servers   29, 50
filing systems, paper   20
front-office activities   18, 19

health and safety   2, 42

IIP (Investors in People Award)   34–5
information-processing systems   ix, x, 16–25, 50–1
   Butlin's Southcoast World   30–4
   Legoland   39
   see also electronic information-processing systems
International Standards Organisation (ISO)   2, 51
Internet   15, 29, 51
Investors in People (IIP)   2–3, 51

INDEX

Kirkham Hotel   viii, 43–7
   analysis of information   46
   arrivals   44
   reservations   44
   restaurant   45–6
   staffing   44

ledgers   20
Legoland vii, viii, 3, 10, 11, 13, 17, 36–42
   administrative systems   37
   admission system   39
   booking system   38–9
   communication systems   40–2
   electronic technology   38–9
   health and safety   42
   information-processing systems   39
   paper based systems   40
   quality standards   42
   staff training   42

Management Information Systems (MIS)   ix, 17–19, 51
manual information-processing systems   19–20, 50

National Vocational Qualifications (NVQs)   35, 51

one-way communication   10–11, 12, 29, 51

paper-based systems   20, 40

quality assurance   2, 51
quality control   2, 51
quality standards   1–2, 51
   Butlin's Southcoast World   34–5
   Legoland   42

report writing   47–8
reservation systems   ix–x, 12, 13–14, 51
   Butlin's Southcoast World   29, 30–3

spreadsheets   21, 50
staff training   35, 42
statutory information   17–18

Training and Enterprise Councils (TECs)   29, 51
two-way communication   11, 12, 29

video-conferencing   41, 51
voice mail   41

wordprocessing software   21, 51